SECOND EDITION

If It Ain't Broke, Fix It!

by

Gil & Vicki Ash

with
Ty Adams

Houston, Texas

OSP PRESS

Published in the United States by Gil & Vicki Ash /

OSP Shooting School, Houston, Texas USA

Publisher's Cataloging-in-Publication
(Provided by Quality Books, Inc.)
Ash, Gil.
    If it ain't broke, fix it!: lessons in shotgunning (and life) /
by Gil & Vicki Ash with Ty Adams. -- 2nd ed.
    p. cm.
    ISBN 0-9760204-0-8

    1. Trapshooting. 2. Shooting.   I. Ash, Vicki.
II. Adams, Ty. III. Title.

GV1181.A84 2004   799.3'132
                         QBI04-700445

Manufactured in the United States of America

Second Edition

Dedication:

To Jerry Meyer for making us believe we could do this.

To Ty Adams for not only capturing the guts of what we teach but the style and humor as well.

To our kids, Andrea and Brian for understanding our passion for what we do.

To our students for their belief and trust in us as we travel the journey together.

To Steve Brown for being a constant source of encouragement, enlightenment, and inspiration to us on our journey.

To Dr. Nancy Kirchmer and her husband Tom for helping us to get our commas in the correct places!

CONTENTS

Foreword/Editor's Note

In many ways, Gil Ash is like a shotgun. He makes a lot of noise, commands attention and respect, and most people are either drawn to him or run from him. You can't help but notice him when he walks into a room, and you wonder how so much energy comes out of such a relatively small package. When his trigger is pulled, he can hit you with five hundred things at once, a steady stream of words coming out like hot metal pellets. Although his words make an impact right away, you won't realize the absolute consistency of their theme until you have a chance to reflect and see the pattern board; all those little nuggets had a common destination. His words work equally well when his target is humor; in fact, that's probably when they work the best. He is the only person I know who can tell a friend she looks like a smurf with a bouffant hairdo and pull it off as a term of endearment. Did I mention he makes a lot of noise?

Even the best shotgun, though, will never hit a target unless it's pointed in the right place. For this to happen, there's got to be someone attached to that gun, someone who is calm when the gun's going off, someone who can handle the noise and the recoil — the attention — someone with perfect focus and remarkable vision. For the shotgun to achieve its fullest potential, there must be a master shooter nearby. Vicki Ash is a master shooter. She is also the only person I know who can point the shotgun that is Gil Ash. Even he will tell you, "I always do what my wife tells me to do … sometimes."

Gil and Vicki Ash are an exciting combination. They can be admired apart, but together they are as fun to watch as a master shooter with a high-dollar Kreighoff. In fact, that's what you'll get when you watch either of them shoot. Although I'm convinced they could teach a monkey with a lazy eye to score well at sporting clays, their teachings have to do with much more than hitting clay targets. It has been my pleasure to work with them on this book, the first of a series, and I think you will see, as I did, that what they teach is applicable not only to shotguns, but to life as well.

Ty Adams

***"**A true shotgunner always reloads
for another try.**"***

INTRODUCTION:
Life is a shotgun

In the beginning, there is light … the result of unseen machinery
set in motion by a gentle hand. The proverbial big bang follows.
Now, whether you're talking about the universe or a shotgun, all
this stuff explodes outward and takes flight into a much larger
space. In the case of the universe, it's a space as big as forever and
colder than a metal toilet seat in a Siberian outhouse. In the case
of a shotgun, it could be a sporting clays course somewhere in
Redneck, Mississippi that probably looks as big as the universe
to a handful of shot. When the pellets fall, some people think
God reloads and it all happens over again. A true shotgunner
always reloads for another try.

We're here to tell you: Life is not a beach, it's a shotgun. On
the seventh day, it probably smelled a lot like gunpowder.

People are the shot. Generation after generation, load after
load, some of us hit what we're aiming at; some of us are stopped
short, while others only graze the target. Some of us miss

completely and land in a pile of cow shit. Most of us start fast and end slow, and at the end of the ride, we all find ourselves rubbing elbows with fish bait. (That's worms for our creatively challenged friends.)

When you live, breathe, and dream shotguns like we do, it's not strange that you start to see life on these terms. Together, we have thirty years of experience teaching others how to hit targets with shotguns and learning from them as much as they learn from us. It's all we do; it's our passion, and we count every day as a blessing because our passion has taken us so far. Gil has been shooting shotguns since childhood, and Vicki started shooting after their marriage, when she decided she'd either have to start shooting or never see her husband. After teaching thousands of students, working with the medical community to understand the physiology and psychology behind shotgunning and sports performance, and learning more on each day of our journey, we have arrived at this book.

Anyone who knows us has found that we aren't shy with our opinions, and we aren't going to be shy here. We believe that short of a cure for ugly, this book has something for everyone.

True, our primary focus is the game of sporting clays, so this will be the primary focus of the book. But, we also think it will offer something to folks participating in skeet and trap, or really any sport involving hitting clay targets with a shotgun. The same principles here also apply to hunting live birds.

This book will not be an exhaustive guide to the history, equipment, apparel, personalities and every other aspect of shotguns and clays sports. It is the first book in a series, a book that will tackle the fundamentals of hitting clay targets. There is no substitution for hands-on instruction, but if you were to come to us for a lesson without ever having pulled the trigger of a shotgun, this is what you would learn.

We tell our students that we represent the shortcut to proficiency, and this is also how we feel about the information in these pages. It's not going to make you taller or shrink your butt or your gut, and it probably won't make you a better shooter just by sleeping with it under your pillow. If you come to it with willingness to change, a positive attitude and a commitment to improve, we believe you will travel the learning curve much faster. And, who knows, if you have a bad attitude, and sleep with it under your pillow, it still might bump up your score a target or two.

So if you've just picked up a shotgun and are looking for a place to start, read on. If you're a tournament shooter looking to review fundamentals or one of our students looking for reference material, read on. If you're looking for a few funny stories and some words of advice that can apply to everyday life, read on. If you're a clays "expert" out of ideas for your next column, read on.

If you're standing in a bookstore trying to soak up our best stuff for free, take this damn thing to the counter and pay for it.

*" If you are not shooting to have fun,
you will not find or achieve much success. "*

CHAPTER 1
Why are you here?

No, we're not going to ask you to give us a reason for existence, but we will ask you to think about why you shoot sporting clays, or whatever shotgun sport you participate in. This is one of the first things we ask our students, and it's something most people don't take time to think about.

Usually the answers include "because it's fun," and they should. Sure, you can have other reasons for participating in a sport, but "because it's fun" should be one of them. It's a great reason. "Because it's fun" is an answer that anyone who has achieved success at anything will likely give you if you ask why they do it. It's the reason for sports, it's the reason for art, and it's a big reason why 250 babies are born every minute.

If you are not shooting to have fun, you will not find or achieve much success.

Fun is what brought us to sporting clays, and it's the reason we teach. Plus, we feel that there is some psychological benefit to breaking things and making noise on a clays range, and we're convinced that you just meet a finer class of people around a shotgun.

Recreational sports allow people to enjoy the risk of winning or losing without the chance of monetary loss, unlike what they face at their jobs every day. It's the adrenaline rush without the risk. People fish, hunt, play tennis, golf, run marathons etc., and as long as they don't put excessive amounts of pressure on themselves to perform, everything is okay. They have fun: win, lose or draw. Problems occur only when you pressure yourself to perform. When this happens, ordinary people get obsessive. ZAP! They regress into whining two-year-olds. They lose perspective. They forget it's just a game.

The frustration of underperformance causes them to do and say things they normally wouldn't do or say. We see this a lot. They throw shells, slam their guns shut, and say things about themselves or their heritage that aren't true and that we're sure their mothers wouldn't appreciate. Smiles turn into frowns. Personality shifts occur in the nicest people. They turn into people you don't want to be around.

The desire to improve drives many people to spend lots of money on gadgets and new equipment in the hopes of improving

Like Mike

Our friend and student Mike Buoy wrote to us a few years back. He found that his shooting had improved dramatically, and this was the reason he gave: "I stopped being so anal about winning. When I felt this emotion kicking in, I stopped and asked myself this question — what will change tomorrow if I don't hit this target? **Nothing***. The sun will still rise." Mike was on to something great here. Sporting clays is a difficult game to master. You will encounter frustration. When you feel yourself getting negative, do what Mike did. Stop and ask yourself "why?" Remind yourself that there is nothing to lose in this game except pride, and even then it's a choice. If you're worried about losing your pride, it's already gone.*

their scores, when all they have to do is relax and have a little fun. It seems simple, but you would be surprised how few people think about this when they encounter problems.

So spend a little time defining why you do this. Write it down! There is something about writing down things like this that helps you keep your perspective.

If the reason you do this is not 100 percent personal (only to please yourself, not others), then you are doing it for the wrong reasons, and your successes, if they happen, will be small and short-lived. Play with the shotgun, dance with the shotgun. Don't be so damn serious.

It is, after all, a game. It's supposed to be fun.

"There is no right way to shoot a shotgun, there are only things that increase or decrease risk."

CHAPTER   2
A word (or two) on eye dominance

Ahhh, yes. One of our favorite subjects. Didn't old Bill Shakespeare write about eye dominance in his play, "Much Ado About Nothing"? Okay, don't twist up your knickers; we do believe that there is such a thing as cross-dominance. We are sure, in fact, that it exists and can cause problems, but it is our experience that the number of people who think they have it is far greater than the number of people who actually have it. What causes the confusion? Take two shooters, one with a true cross-dominance problem, and one with no cross-dominance problem who has fallen into the habit of looking at the barrel of the gun, checking the lead instead of focusing on the target, and they will display the same symptoms. So, a common problem with technique can masquerade as a cross-dominance problem, especially if the shooter doesn't want to believe he or she has a technique problem.

For those of you who are new to the sport, allow us to explain.

The ideal situation when shooting a shotgun is to have the gun shouldered on the same side as the master or dominant eye.

If you are right-handed and have a left dominant eye, when you mount the gun your brain will want to reference the point of the gun with your dominant eye, caus-ing you to "cross fire." If you suspect you have a dominance problem, seek profes-sional help from an experienced coach!

IF IT AIN'T BROKE, FIX IT!

We all have one dominant eye, just like we are right- or left-handed. It is the eye that leads the other to focus. We call it cross-dominance when you shoot right-handed but have a dominant left eye, or vice versa. We're addressing this here, at the beginning of the book, because there seems to be a hefty amount of misinformation about cross-dominance and how we coaches deal with the problem. To make matters worse, there is the feared intermittent cross-dominance, which makes everybody worry their master eye could suddenly switch.

We are not saying that eye dominance plays a small role in shooting accuracy. That would be incorrect and foolish. In an ideal situation, the gun should be shouldered on the same side as the master, or dominant eye. In some situations, this does not or cannot happen, and for decades cross-dominant shooters have been instructed to close or "patch" the dominant eye. We, however, have been successful in helping hundreds of people with cross-dominance learn to shoot with both eyes open, without switching shoulders.

We have also mastered this technique in our own shooting, and can shoot from either shoulder with both eyes open because the system we teach has evolved from our research and from our journey to understand vision and how the brain interprets what we see. It is now our understanding that eye dominance plays a much bigger role in success or failure if the shooter looks for what we call "conscious lead." We'll expand on this later, but let us say for now that if a shooter learns to focus beyond the barrels, on the front edge of the target, letting the subconscious mind calculate the right lead, then eye dominance becomes much less of a factor and less of a problem.

If you are cross-dominant, you will not learn how to shoot with both eyes open in this book. It takes hands-on instruction and a lot of practice. Even with instruction, you may not be able to overcome the challenge of true cross-dominance. It's a lot like the golfer who went to his pro with a horrible slice. After instruction, he understood what caused the problem and what he needed to do to fix it. He then asked how long it would take to fix the problem. The pro answered, "Maybe a week, maybe a month, maybe a year, maybe never. But you will never know unless you try."

It is a challenge, but there are alternative solutions to cross-dominance, other than eye occlusions, and we have had success with those alternatives in our teachings.

The self-diagnosed and the misdiagnosed come to us in hoards. They wear eye patches or tape one side of their glasses, or maybe they shoot with one eye shut, or start with two eyes open, get a fix on the target and then shut one eye, and sometimes they just squint one eye a little bit. Usually what we do in these instances is lay a hand on their foreheads, remove the patches or tear the tape from their glasses, and holler, "You're healed!"

At the very least, we ask them to consider removing the tape or trying to shoot with both eyes open, if just for the day.

Why? Well, let's think about this a little bit. If the doctor told you there was a condition in your arm that might cause it to lose strength once in a while, would you ask him to amputate? Would you tie it behind your back and do everything with the other arm? Does the fact that you are more coordinated with one arm than the other prevent you from swinging a golf club or a baseball bat?

Eye dominance simply means that one eye leads the other to focus. On objects at a distance, they work together and still focus together. If cross-dominance made that much difference, you wouldn't be able to ride a bicycle or drive a car; you'd be knocking things over all the time.

Can you achieve a certain amount of success shooting with tape, a patch, or one eye closed? Yes. Is it better to shoot with both eyes open? Yes. The targets will look larger and closer and appear to move more slowly. This has been proven to us over and over, even in our own shooting.

We have taught many people who only have the use of one eye, and they are able to shoot well because they are used to looking at the world with only one eye. If you have two eyes, though, you are used to looking at the world with both eyes. If you close one, you're giving your brain incorrect information about how to hit a four-inch disc at exactly the time when you are supposed to shoot it. The disc is hard enough to see with both eyes, now you want to see it with only one? If you find the target with both eyes and then shut one eye, you've given the brain two different sight pictures. You have gone from seeing the target at a specific distance, speed, and size, to seeing a target that looks farther away, faster, and smaller. Let's not make this any harder than it is, people. Closing one eye mid-shot creates doubt in your move and prevents you from trusting your breakpoint. It also hinders your ability to pick up targets on the side of the occluded or closed eye.

Okay, we're going to tell you something here that you might not be able to handle right now, but that's okay, because we don't mind repeating ourselves. Ready? Here it is: More targets are missed due to lack of target focus (looking at the lead), improper gun speed (moving too fast), and a poor mount (mounting the gun to the shoulder first, not the face) than all the other reasons combined.

We'll talk more about this in Chapter 18, but for now we'll venture to say that nine times out of ten, if you're missing targets and you don't know why, at least one of these three reasons is the culprit, not cross-dominance.

Even if you truly do have a cross-dominance problem (and have been diagnosed as cross-dominant by a doctor or optometrist) the system we teach will allow you to overcome it. You will encounter frustration, and if you are used to shooting with one eye closed, it will take some time to retrain your brain. But if you make the commitment and put in the practice, you will achieve more success with two eyes than you can with one.

Our advice if you're a beginner in this sport, especially if you never plan to become a tournament shooter, is to not trouble yourself with whether you're right- or left-eye dominant. Don't try to self-diagnose. Just go out and start shooting targets. Try to use both eyes. (It's our experience, you are going to close an eye and try to aim anyway!) Learn a smooth move and mount. (The move and mount is simply the act of bringing the gun from a lowered "ready" position to the "firing" position against the shoulder and face.) If you keep getting better and keep pushing through plateaus and slumps, don't ever worry about dominance. If you don't get better, go take a lesson.

If you're serious about tournament shooting, we advise starting your training with an experienced instructor who understands the eyes and the brain, how they are connected, and how they run the body. From there you can determine your dominance and go over your options.

If you've been shooting for a while and you encounter consistent problems, and you suspect you have a cross-dominance problem, you have several choices. First

Vicki Talks

*I am left-eye dominant and right-handed. I now shoot right-handed with both eyes open. I wore an eye patch on my left eye to shoot, but it was difficult to walk around, and the targets looked smaller, faster, and farther away. I decided to make the change to shooting with both eyes open. People told me for years that I wouldn't be able to do it. It did take some time and it was frustrating, but it really helped my shooting. Once I had retrained my brain, I was able to score right up there with the right-eyed and right-handed folks. There will be people (even some "expert instructors") who will read this and say it can't be done. What they are really saying is **they** can't do it. I've done it. Gil has done it. We have helped hundreds of people who are cross-dominant learn to shoot with both eyes open. Is it the only answer? No. Is it a viable alternative to closing or patching the eye? Yes. Can everyone do it? No. Is it easy to do? Sometimes yes, and sometimes no. For me, it worked. It might for you, too.*

IF IT AIN'T BROKE, FIX IT!

confirm to yourself that you are not looking for conscious lead before you pull the trigger. People who shoot conscious lead (checking the bird/barrel relationship *before* they pull the trigger) have a far greater problem with cross-dominance than those who don't. If you can learn to focus on the *front* of the target and let your subconscious insert the muzzle in the lead, cross-dominance is less of a problem. Some people who are cross-dominant switch shoulders and retrain themselves to shoot from the shoulder on the same side as the dominant eye. Some people close an eye or occlude the non-shooting eye with tape. We advocate shooting with both eyes open always. If you have a dominance problem, find an experienced coach to help you with it. The mental aspect of shotgun games is huge, and if you can't get past the fact that you're cross-dominant, you should do whatever is necessary to put your mind at ease. The last thing you want to do is self-diagnose and self-coach yourself through an eye dominance problem. Get experienced help!

Ultimately, the decision is up to you. It leads back to what we discussed in the first chapter. The reason you shoot should determine how much you put into getting better. If you've been shooting with one eye closed for 20 years, shoot consistently in the 60s, and you just want to go out on a clays range with your friends, shoot in the 70s and enjoy your afternoon, keep shooting with one eye and have fun. We can get you to the 70s without making you open both eyes. But expecting to win tournaments as a one-eyed shooter is a whole different matter.

We tell our students there is no right and wrong in this game except with regard to focus, which is either there or not. For everything else there is no right and wrong, there are only things that increase or decrease risk. Shooting with one eye closed or blurred by tape increases risk, but if you can't get past cross-dominance mentally and it makes you happy to shoot with one eye, shoot with one eye. If you want to switch shoulders, switch shoulders. Hell, if it really makes you happy to shoot blindfolded in your underwear, and if you could do so safely, we'd be all for it. Just don't expect to hit many targets.

wire. *As the peripheral and focal vision carry that information along the optic nerve, they travel along their own little pathways. They're not commingled as they converge at the visual cortex where it's like grand central station and this visual information goes to all the different parts of the brain. What I discovered about shooting, the key thing that I put together, was this: focal vision goes from your retina to your motor center in immeasurable time. Faster than we can measure. But the information from your peripheral vision takes about three-tenths of a second to get to the visual cortex."*

So peripheral vision is taking a slower train to your motor center than focal vision. But what does this mean to shotgun shooters?

"Well, a shooter can only focus on one thing at a time," Steve said. "And the visual information from that one thing will reach his brain faster than everything else in the peripheral, which is delayed three-tenths of a second. So if he's shooting with the method of exact lead, he is trying to focus on the barrel, the lead and the target all at the same time. His priority is to focus on that lead ahead of the

target, so the target falls to the periphery. When the target is in the periphery and he pulls the trigger, he is pulling the trigger based on delayed information. For the three-tenths of a second that it took that information to get to his motor center, the target kept moving. If the target had been in his focal vision, he would have perceived the target in real time. That's where the method [Gil and Vicki] teach has the advantage. In that method, the instinctive shooter's eyes are focused acutely on the front of the target the entire time; that's the priority, not exact lead. So the instinctive shooter will pull the trigger based on more accurate visual information."

Steve said the real payoff for him is that he now understands why, if three of his master class buddies are shooting the same station, one of them might say he ran the station giving the target eight feet of lead and the other two might say they ran it with only a few inches of lead. "Someone once told me, perception is reality," Steve said. "Well, amen to that!"

[1]Dr. Wayne F. Martin, O.D., *An Insight to Sports*, p.22

"The only experience worthwhile is the successful or unsuccessful execution of a plan."

CHAPTER 3
Breakpoint, step one of any method

Before we get into the fundamentals of the move and the mount, it's important that you understand the system we teach, because your move and mount is dependent on the system you employ to break targets. There are many methods employed in shotgun sports — swing-through, pull away, maintained lead, sustained lead, yadda, yadda, yadda — and they all have different risks, which we will illustrate later.

We will teach our students any method they want to learn, but the method we advocate and use ourselves is one we have developed over many years of shooting and instruction. It's the system we're going to show you before we get into any of the others. We think it's the method with the least amount of risk (it is good for more than one or two types of targets), it is the most forgiving (you don't need to have impeccable timing to succeed with it), and it's just the best method we have found for the game of sporting clays where there is an infinite variety of targets. It works equally well in hunting fields and for games with target consistency like skeet and trap.

We're not big on names, so our method doesn't have one. You can call it whatever you like. Our suggestions: The Ash Method, The Sweet Ash Method, The Kick Ash Method, The Best Method (El Método Mejor for those who prefer foreign flavor), or The Mother Of All Methods.

Whatever you want to call it, our method begins with breakpoints, and we'd argue that any method you employ should begin with breakpoints. A breakpoint is simply a spot in the flight path of the target where you intend to break it. This is critical. Before you even shut your gun and address the target, you should know exactly where you want to break the target. If you haven't seen the target when you get in the stand, ask to see it. As you watch its flight pick a point, relative to something else, where you will break it. This breakpoint could be a tree in the distance, a boulder, or just above a distinct pile of wood; the more specific you are, the better. You can't have timing without picking a breakpoint.

This doesn't mean that you say, "Okay, I'm going to break it in the sweet spot, just before it starts to fall," because you don't have a concrete point of reference. Also, if you say you're going to hit a target just before it starts to fall, you're going to miss it more often than not because the only way you can tell it's about to fall is by seeing it's already on the way down. So pick a specific point in the flight path of the target to break it.

Three Different Places

The sweet spot of a target is generally somewhere near the middle of the flight path, where it begins losing power. It is fine if you learn to take targets at the sweet spot, as most everybody does, and for the beginning of your learning curve, most of the breakpoints you choose should be in the sweet spot. If you're going to play sporting clays, though, you must learn to break every type of target in three different places — sweet, late and early. Don't try to move the breakpoint when you are still developing your move and mount, but be aware that you will not always be able to take the targets where they're sweet.

Once you've picked a breakpoint, you have to commit to it. When the target gets there, have the gun mounted and pull the trigger. Even if somewhere during the swing you think you picked the wrong breakpoint, pull the trigger anyway. If you don't, it defeats the point of having a breakpoint, which is to eliminate doubt and allow for better shot analysis. Even if the breakpoint you choose is not the best for the target, if you are decisive with it and you miss, you will know it doesn't work and can change it. If you aren't decisive, you won't know what to change.

" The shooter who remains in perfect balance through the shot can move the gun precisely and consistently, regardless of target line or speed."

CHAPTER 4
Stance

Once you know where you're going to break the target, it's time to address the field from the stand. It is important to put your feet in the correct position in relation to the breakpoint so you will be in balance with it. Point your left foot (right foot for lefties) just to the right of the breakpoint you've picked. The other foot should never be parallel to the front foot, but should be placed to the side and at an angle. It should not be a 90-degree angle, but slightly less, maybe 65 to 70 degrees. If you're not good at geometry, just hold your hand out in front of your crotch, palm toward the ground, with your fingers and your thumb neither spread completely out nor held in tight. Now match the angle the outside of your hand makes.

The heel of the back foot should be 8-12 inches from the heel of the front foot. There should be a straight line between the heel of the back foot, the front toe or ball of your front foot, and the breakpoint. Your feet should be just under a shoulder-width apart

A line from your rear heel across your front toe or ball of your front foot should line up with your breakpoint.

IF IT AIN'T BROKE, FIX IT!

A quick and easy visual reference point can be made by placing your wrist in front of your crotch and lining up your feet with each side of your hand.

or about the same distance apart as your armpits. If they get too much wider, you won't be able to move to the bird as well. With an overly wide stance, if the wind comes up you won't be able to make an adjustment in the swing as easily. Try it and see if you don't believe us. Put your feet really far apart and try to make a good gun mount on an imaginary crossing target. Not easy, is it? Now try it with the weight on the front foot in an armpit-width stance and see if it makes a difference. With the feet in this stance, the gun is able to move to your face easily and you have a good foundation for a smooth mount.

Again, your feet should never be parallel; this locks up your hips and makes a crossing move or quick quartering move nearly impossible. Once the feet are in the correct position, you should be standing straight with only a slight lean forward over the front

The beginning point for correct foot position: 1. Heels a little less than shoulder width apart, 2. Toes slightly farther apart than heels.

Your weight should be on your front foot.

A stance that is too wide has more than one pivot point during the swing.

A wide stance encourages excessive body movement and balance becomes a problem during the shot.

IF IT AIN'T BROKE, FIX IT!

foot. Your nose should be just over the toes of this foot. The spine should have just a slight bend forward in the upper back and your weight should be on the ball of the front foot. A good, consistent mount is impossible with the weight on the back foot because weight displacement determines the line of your natural swing. With weight on the back foot, your natural swing will be a rainbow, but the only thing in the pot at the end of it will be your shot. You won't hit many targets with a swing like this.

With the weight on the front foot, your cheek is ahead of your shoulder pocket, and the gun can easily slide up to your cheek and your shoulder at the same time. Also, with the weight on your front foot, you only have one pivot point; with weight distributed evenly between both feet, you have two pivot points and consistency becomes impossible. It's like driving a car with all the tires out of balance. When your body does anything but pivot on one point, the gun speed and line are affected in a negative way.

Balance is crucial. If at any time during the swing your body loses balance, one of two decisions will be made by your subconscious mind:

1. Keep swinging with the bird and fall down.

2. Keep balance and stand up by letting the gun either stop or come off line with the target.

A New Stance

Dan Whitehead, one of our students in California, recently helped Gil underscore the importance of foot position. As Gil watched Dan shoot in the morning, he noticed that Dan was holding his feet nearly parallel. Instead of mentioning it right away, Gil wanted to see just how much difference it was making in Dan's shooting. In the afternoon Dan was having particular trouble on a quick quartering shot. After trying several self-corrections, Dan asked Gil for advice, and Gil suggested that he open up his stance, not a lot, just a few inches. Dan made the slight stance correction and nailed the station from there on out. He broke the target on every shot with the new stance and helped make a memorable point. Stance counts.

Guess which one will happen every time? Your balance instinct is a self-preservation instinct and it's your strongest instinct. The gun will come off line for the same reason that your hands come out when you fall forward. If you can fall flat on your face without putting your hands out, you can come to one of our clinics, and we'll give you fifty bucks and let you shoot any way you want.

In order for the swing to be consistent, the body must remain in balance. The shooter who remains in perfect balance through the shot can move the gun precisely and consistently regardless of target line or speed. This basic stance allows balance. There are some advanced target presentations that require a slightly different stance, but we won't address those circumstances right now. Until you've mastered the basics, stay focused on the basic stance.

Now, in the stand, once you've got your feet set and your body in the right position, don't think any more about it. The goal is to make the mechanics of the shot a function of the subconscious mind. Practice the stance until you no longer have to think about it.

*"You should be mentally focused
but physically relaxed before you call 'pull.'"*

CHAPTER 5
Grip

Let us give you a picture we see so often in our classes. The student gets into the stand (usually this manifests itself in men) and boy, does he look focused. His jaw is set; his mouth is pursed. He's got that gun in a white-knuckle death grip. He's holding it like it's the ticket to salvation. He's puckered up so tight you could feed him coal and he'd make you a diamond. When he calls "pull," he jerks the gun to his face and almost always moves faster than the target. Slow, floating crossers just ruin this guy.

The problem here is that our friend has mistaken being tense for being focused. Don't make this mistake. You should be mentally focused but physically relaxed before you call "pull." The first place tension will show up is in the grip.

The grip is simple and should be the same for everyone. If you're right-handed, your left hand is placed on the forend of the gun. Point your index finger along the side of the barrel. Don't

Gripping the forend of the shotgun with all your fingers wrapped around the stock creates excessive muscle tension in the left arm and shoulder.

It is easy to feel this tension by just holding your hand out in front of your body like this. Note the position of the hand and fingers.

By simply pointing your index finger straight ahead, you can feel the tension leave your arm and shoulder. Note the position of the hand and fingers.

IF IT AIN'T BROKE, FIX IT!

To correctly grip the forend of your shotgun:
1. Point your index finger and place it on the side of the forend parallel to the barrel.

2. Rest the gun in the remaining 3 fingers.

point your finger underneath the barrel of the gun because this is not the way you normally point at something. Let the bulk of the gun rest in your three remaining fingers with your palm on the side. Remember, you want the gun to feel like an extension of your arm. The arm and hand should be relaxed. Don't squeeze the gun much harder than you would squeeze a tube of toothpaste to bring the toothpaste to the edge of the hole.

The back hand, or right hand for the right-handers, should also be relaxed and the index finger ready to pull the trigger. The grip pressure with the right hand should be the same as the left. The only job of the back hand is to lift the gun to your face and shoulder and then pull the trigger. If the back hand moves faster than the front hand, it's going to seesaw the barrels, and you'll probably miss because the gun will come to your shoulder first,

The back hand grip position is critical for consistent mounting of the gun. The curve in the pistol grip tends to position the hand too high on the grip. It's comfortable to hold with the hand high. It is also comfortable to carry in the field. The problem is that it is almost impossible to mount the gun to your face when gripped this way. See photo opposite page.

The simplest way to achieve the correct grip position is to simply slide your rear hand straight into the grip and trigger from the rear of the gun.

With the hand lower in the grip, the gun can easily be mounted consistently to the face and shoulder.

The wrists can remain straight and strong through the mount and shot. See photo opposite page.

IF IT AIN'T BROKE, FIX IT!

When the back hand position is high in the grip and the gun is mounted, the right wrist is cocked at an angle. This keeps the gun from getting to the anchor point which is always the cheek.

The ideal position when the gun is mounted is for both wrists to be straight and the elbows to be at about a 45 degree angle from the swing plane of the gun. This allows for the greatest amount of strength and mobility in the hands, arms and shoulders when moving, mounting and shooting a shotgun.

and then your cheek. If the gun gets to the shoulder and then to the face, the face must move to the gun. If your face is moving down to the gun, your focus goes off the target. Relax. If you are tense, you are more apt to have a bad gun mount. If a muscle is tense, it must first relax before it can move. If you will start out relaxed, you won't lose that valuable time to get to the target. Your move will be smoother and you will get to the bird faster, a good gun mount will occur, and your chances for a hit are better. Another tidbit of information — if you are tense, your eyes tense up also. You must see the bird. That's the number one thing required of a shooter. If your eyes are tense and you can't see the bird well, you will have a harder time hitting it.

Try squinting your eyes and focusing on something … it's harder to see, isn't it?

So remember to relax that death grip you have on the gun. Make sure all the muscles in both arms and shoulders are in a neutral state so that you can respond to the motion of the bird as it comes into your view. Be calm. It's not going to shoot back.

Muscle Tension

A tense muscle must first relax before it can move. To illustrate this, put your hand flat on a table in front of you. Push down on the table. Try to raise your hand slowly off the table. Do you feel the tense muscles relaxing before you can lift your hand? Now softly place the same hand in the same place on the table. Don't push down, just stay in contact with the table. Slowly raise your hand. See how smooth the move was? The muscles were in a neutral state, so they were free to expand and contract, creating a smooth and flowing move. How loose is loose enough? On a scale of one to 10, a two or a three works best. If one is your hand laying on the table like soft scrambled eggs, and 10 is pushing down as hard as your weight will allow, somewhere between a two or three with both hands is a good level for your grip.

If It Ain't Broke, Fix It!

*"We don't cut our eyes when we're
taking a look at a bubbly blonde or a
tall-dark-and-handsome, so we shouldn't cut
our eyes to focus on the clay target."*

CHAPTER 6
Focal point

The focal point is a location in your field of vision where you will
hold your eyes still before calling "pull." Of course, it's going to
vary from target presentation to target presentation, but in general,
you should find a spot close enough to the trap so you can quickly
focus on the target with plenty of time to make your move and
mount. If you find a spot too close to the trap to let your eyes settle,
you will be chasing the target and won't be able to obtain laser-like
focus on it. If you choose a spot too far out, you might be able to
focus on the target, but you won't have time to read, move, mount
and shoot the target in the chosen breakpoint.

When you find your spot, pick an object out past the flight
path of the target and let your eyes settle on it. It could be a leaf,
a tree, a branch, a cloud, anything that you can focus on that's
farther out than the flight path of the target. This is important.
If you pick something to focus on that is between you and the

target, it will take you longer to focus on the target when it appears in the picture.

Don't believe it? You can prove it anywhere. Pick two objects, one farther away than the other. Focus first on the far object then bring your eyes into focus on the near object. Did you feel how it snaps into focus with just one move? Now focus on the near object first and then focus on the one farther out. Did you feel your eyes make two moves? First they found the object, and then they focused on it, right? Good, then the case is settled and science class is over.

So once you've found your object beyond the flight path, focus there and keep your eyes very calm and still. If you do this, you'll be able to focus on the front edge of the target as soon as your eyes detect target motion.

Ideal focal points will also differ from person to person. What is right for your buddy might not be right for you. Your best focal point will depend on which side the target comes from and also is relative to the side of your eye dominance and whether you are right-brain or left-brain dominant. Experiment with different focal points on targets coming from the right and left. See whether it is better for you to look at the trap or in front of the trap. Some of you will find a difference, some of you will not, but it is a good idea to analyze which focal points work best for you on specific presentations. Gil must look away from the trap, beyond the flight path on any target coming from the left. When they come from the right he is better off looking at the trap, or even behind it. He sees the target cleaner and quicker that way. For Vicki, it is just the opposite. We'll save a tree and abstain from going into the physiology of this, because even once you understand it, you'll still have to experiment and see what works best for you. Believe us, there is a difference for each person.

Point your nose where you look.
When setting up to call for the target, never cut your eyes to pick up the target. Always point your nose at your focal point. The target will be sharper sooner.

Even so, what we've found over the years is not that people are missing because they haven't chosen a focal point that is right for them — they are missing because they do not have still, calm eyes when they call "pull." We've found that the most frequent cause of a miss for intermediate to advanced shooters is that they're moving their eyes when they call "pull," anticipating the target.

The higher the quality input (picture on your brain), the better the output (how you move to that picture). The better the focus, the better the move.

One last thing to remember: Point your nose wherever your focal point is. This might seem like common sense but a lot of people feel like they have to keep their heads still and then cut their eyes back toward the trap. Don't cut your eyes back. Turn your head over the gun. Point your nose at the focal point. As the target emerges your eyes will lock on. While you watch it float across the sky, you will find you are tracking the target with your nose. Try it, you'll see that your eyes focus over your nose — gentlemen, this is why your wife always catches you when you're focusing on something you shouldn't.

We don't cut our eyes when we're taking a look at a bubbly blonde or a tall-dark-and-handsome, so we shouldn't cut our eyes to focus on the clay target.

"Exactly how you hold the gun before you call 'pull' is a matter of comfort and preference in most cases."

CHAPTER   7
Hold point

As you address the target presentation and settle into your stance, the hold point is where the muzzle is pointed; it's where you hold the gun before you call "pull." Like the focal point, the hold point will vary from presentation to presentation. In fact, it should correspond to the area you have chosen for a breakpoint.

Here's a general rule we use: On a quartering shot, the hold point should be halfway between the focal point and the breakpoint, just under the flight path of the bird. It's a rule of halves. If you pick a breakpoint that is sweet or late, the hold point will be splitting the distance. If you pick an early breakpoint, the hold point will be closer to the breakpoint and just under the line. There will be less time to insert the gun. The move must be shorter and directly to the breakpoint. Speed comes from the efficiency of the move, not how fast you swing. When shooting an earlier breakpoint, the focal point is critical. You must be able to see the target quickly to shoot it quickly.

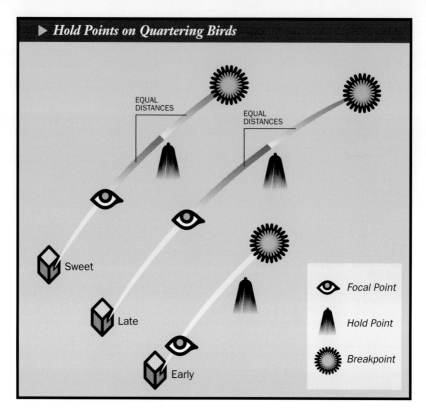

Hold Points on Quartering Birds

EQUAL DISTANCES

EQUAL DISTANCES

Sweet

Late

Early

Focal Point

Hold Point

Breakpoint

Hold points on quartering birds shot sweet or late should be halfway between the focal point and the breakpoint, just under the line of the bird. When breaking the quartering bird early, the hold point will be much closer to the breakpoint and just under the line. The focal point is critical. You must be able to see it quickly to shoot it quickly. When shot early, the target will be fast and there will be very little time to move the gun. The move must be shorter and more efficient and directly to the breakpoint. Speed comes from the efficiency of the move, not how fast you swing.

The rule is two-thirds for crossing targets. The hold point will be closer to the breakpoint than with a quartering target. Instead of half the distance, it will be one-third of the distance from the breakpoint and two-thirds from the focal point, giving you more time for a soft initial move to the breakpoint — a longer period to get in sync with the target.

Just so you'll know, a crossing shot is defined as any shot that crosses in front of the shooter at a 90-degree angle. A quartering

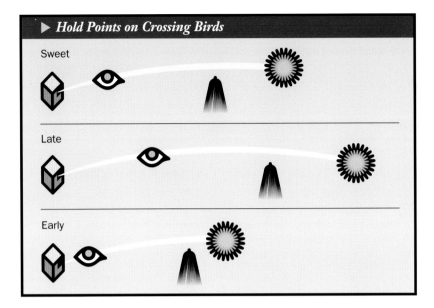

Hold Points on Crossing Birds

Sweet

Late

Early

Hold points on crossing birds shot sweet or late should be about 1/3 back from the breakpoint to the focal point. The muzzles should be just under the line. This allows for plenty of time to focus on the target and a soft, gradual beginning of the lateral move to the breakpoint with the muzzles.

When shooting the crossing bird early, the focal point is critical. You must be able to see it quickly to shoot it quickly. The hold point will be much closer to the breakpoint and just under the line. When shot early, the target will be fast and there will be very little time to move the gun. The move must be shorter, more efficient, and directly to the breakpoint! If not, the target will overtake the gun and you will be behind. Again, speed comes from the efficiency of the move, not how fast you swing! When shot early, all targets take more lead than you think. You must learn to trust it!

presentation occurs when the target moves toward or away from the shooter.

Some shooters prefer to start with a mounted gun, and while this is illegal in some clay sports, it's not illegal in sporting clays. We don't recommend it, though, and it is not part of the system we teach. It puts you at a disadvantage from the start by splitting your field of vision. This makes focus more difficult and makes it infinitely harder to develop feel with the target. Also, nearly every target thrown at you on a clays range gives you enough time that you can move to it from an unmounted position. The only exceptions to this are extreme quartering shots. In our video,

Mechanics

We want to drop a little bomb on you right in the middle of all this mechanical talk. The keys to our teachings are mechanical excellence, extreme mental focus, and trust. Obviously, you need mechanical excellence before you can have true focus and before you can trust in your mechanics, but we think some level of focus and trust can be learned while you are mastering mechanics. We will be repeating this, but it is critical: You need to eventually get past mechanical thinking. It is a necessary evil at the beginning of the learning curve, but we find that too many people get caught up in thinking mechanically after they already have a smooth move and mount. We want to warn you about this here so you can't say we didn't tell you.

As you learn the mechanics of the shot, try to concentrate more on your body and less on what the gun is doing. Feel is very important.

The more time you spend thinking about what the gun is doing, the worse you will shoot. Just try to make the gun a natural extension of your arms. When you begin to feel that connection (when the mechanics begin to feel natural) you have to wean yourself off mechanical thinking, especially when you are competing or practicing competitively. During mechanical practice, it's okay to think about mechanics, but you will need to foster a mind that's empty of technique and mechanics when you're shooting for score. We find that way too many people get hung up on the trip the gun is making and lose sight of where it's going.

To take your shooting to the next level, focus on the destination, and the trip will take care of itself. You'll hit more targets and have a lot more fun.

Best I can remember, being at Gramma's house was always more fun than getting there!

"Strategy and How to Play the Game," we go through the various occurrences where shooting with a mounted gun is recommended. For the purpose of learning a fundamental move, however, we advise against it.

Don't select a hold point where the gun is blocking the flight path on those targets that are presented on the six o'clock to twelve o'clock lines. This means targets like teal thrown vertically and straight outgoers and straight incomers, both from under your feet and over your head.

With the gun held on the target's line, the shooting eye is blocked, which results in the shooter seeing the gun. This leads to cross-firing (another word for the dreaded intermittent cross-dominance) and flinching, both induced by excessive muzzle awareness. Get the gun out of your face so you can focus on the target.

For these targets it's important that you don't block your view of the target with the gun. If you're right-handed, select a hold point where the gun is a little more to the right side; if left-handed, go left.

Exactly how you hold the gun before you call "pull" is a matter of comfort and preference in most cases. Again, we don't want to teach you to shoot exactly like we do; hell, we don't even shoot exactly alike. Find a position to hold the gun that feels good to you. Most shooters hold the butt of the gun just below and slightly in front of their armpits with the muzzles pointed toward the target flight path. This means muzzles high on a high bird and muzzles low on a low bird. We've already mentioned that you don't want to hold the gun where it will block the flight path of the target, and down the line we'll mention another exception or two, where holding the gun in a slightly different place for certain targets will decrease risk in your shot. For now, just find one place where you will hold the gun for most targets. Groove it so it's the same every time. Let it be your default setting.

If your hold point on any target on the 6 to 12 o'clock line is on the line, you will see the target with your non-shooting eye first. This creates a long list of visual problems that result in missed targets.

If you will move your hold point to the side of the line, you can pick up and focus on the target with both eyes. How far? Far enough so that you can see the target with BOTH eyes in your focal point!

IF IT AIN'T BROKE, FIX IT!

A Good Howell 2003

In May of 2003, we had the pleasure of talking with Mick Howell on our Coaching Hour show. Mick won the Browning Briley World and the World English Sporting Clays Tournaments back-to-back in April of 2003.

On the show, Mick told us how he learned to shoot trap with a mounted gun and how he shot that way for many years until he decided to take on sporting clays. To our surprise, even though he has had enormous success, Mick said he's never really felt like he's had a good gun mount.

"I don't get the gun up as high as maybe I should … and that is a throwback to those days when I used to shoot trap and pre-mount the gun," he said. "If there's one thing I could improve, that's what it would be."

Mick went on to say that he believes some of the younger shooters who have very fluid low gun mounts (and insert the gun in the lead as we teach) will elevate the game to a higher level. "I think that's a very, very efficient way of shooting," he said, "and if I were starting over, that would be the way that I would try and go. I would certainly try to get out and watch those guys who shoot like that and try and model my own shooting around them if I could."

As it is now, Mick holds the gun a little higher than most sporting clays shooters, a holdover from his trapshooting days. Now, we have a real hard time saying that 40 is old, but that's what Mick said: If he wasn't so old, he would learn to shoot with a lower gun mount.

We asked again, just to make sure.

"Yeah, I would," he said in reiteration. "I would clear the gun away from my face a little bit more."

We would urge you to get the CD with the entire discussion, available at www.ospschool.com.

*"Our system is based on this premise:
Be sloppy in lead, precise in focus. If you're worried
about lead, you'll end up looking at the gun
and not the target."*

CHAPTER 8
The "L" word and your move

It's time to call "pull." You have an excellent pre-shot routine, and you have excellent pre-shot mechanics. You have picked a breakpoint and are ready to commit to it no matter what happens along the move and mount. You have a solid, balanced stance that will allow you to track the bird precisely. Your grip pressure is equal in both hands — confident, but not white-knuckle. **Both eyes** are focused and still, held on an object you've chosen, ready to go to the front edge of the target as it emerges. You are holding the gun in a comfortable way with the muzzles pointed at a spot in relation to the breakpoint and focal point. You are relaxed physically and alert mentally. It's time to call "pull."

The question is, how do you move to the target? Or better said, how do you move in relation to the target, letting it come to you instead of trying to chase it? Where do you insert the gun? How much lead do you give it, or how far in front of the target should you insert the gun? How precise does it have to be? What happens if you miss? How will you deal with the comments if you do? What if you are a total failure at this sport? Did you remember to turn off the stove?

These are just a few things that run through a beginning shooter's mind, but the biggest is usually that damn "L" word: Lead. Everybody wants to know about lead. What about the lead? Well, we want you to forget about lead for a while, and precise lead forever. Our system is based on this premise: Be sloppy in lead, precise in focus. If you're worried about lead, you'll end up looking at the gun and not the target.

We'll get into our zone version of lead later, but right now we want to give you some mental pictures. The first is a description of the move and mount of our student Craig Hill as he shoots a 25-yard crosser. Craig's move is our idea of the perfect move and mount, a prime example of the Sweet Ash Method as seen in our "How to Practice and Understanding the Move" video.

Of course, your actual move and mount will be slightly different from Craig's, and it should be. Trying to replicate exactly the move and mount of any person or description is silly because your body is different and your brain is different. This description should be a template, a basic guide to a quality move and mount using our method. It's not set in stone, and we encourage you to take it and develop your own rhythm and style. Here it is:

The target is a slow floater, crossing from left to right. Craig's eyes are still as he calls "pull," and as the target enters his field of vision, he begins to move. First, his head begins turning with the target, allowing him to focus on the front edge. Shortly after, if not at the same time, his hands slowly begin moving laterally, from left to right, with the target. His first move is lateral, not up and then lateral. There is more movement in his lead hand (moving left to right) than his back hand (moving right to left and bringing the stock up toward his face).

*Because the hold point starts out in front of the target, Craig's gun is still pointed in front of the target as it gains ground. The gun is moving slower than the target, but as the target is losing speed, Craig is gradually speeding up, slowly matching the muzzle speed to the target speed. Now his hands are moving laterally and up toward the mount, toward his face. The gun is still in front of the bird. There is very little body movement until the mount is complete, and even then only a slight swiveling of the shoulders from left to right. As the bird approaches his predetermined breakpoint, the movement of his hands (with the gun as an extension) mirrors the movement and speed of the bird. He **feels** a bodily connection to the target. He lets the bird come to the gun, never moving the gun faster than the bird, but never letting the bird get in front of the gun. Finishing the move, he brings the gun to his face (**not** his head to the gun), focusing on the front of the bird as it merges with the muzzles at the breakpoint. The following things happen at almost exactly the same time: the gun touches his face … the barrels reach the breakpoint just ahead of the bird … he pulls the trigger. That thing is powder, Bubba.*

Notice the things Craig did not do. He did not move the gun up to his shoulder, put his head down on it, and then swing through the bird from behind. He moved it laterally with his front hand first, toward the breakpoint the whole time, and always in front of the bird. ***He did not, at any point, look at the barrel.*** He did not check the lead (the distance between the barrel and the bird.) All of his focus was from the barrel out; all of his focus was on the target. He did not move the gun or any part of his body faster than the bird. It was the fastest object in the picture at all times.

These are the basics of the move we advocate for our students, and we stress getting this right before anything else. You will never shoot better than the quality of your basic move and mount. It's a thousand times more important than lead, which we feel will take care of itself once a quality move is obtained. Before moving on, go back and re-read the description of Craig's move. Try to dissect it into slow motion, and as you read each sentence, make the move along with the description, visualizing a target in front of you.

Our video, "How To Practice and Understanding the Move," provides a good visual example of a quality move on both crossing and quartering targets.

It is much easier to understand this move by watching someone do it than by reading a description, but we'd like to give you another mental picture to help you understand it. Imagine this:

You are in a car idling at a stoplight and preparing to enter the onramp to a freeway. The cars on the freeway are going 70 mph, which looks really fast from your stopped position. The light turns green, and as you enter the onramp, you see heavy traffic, but as you look over your shoulder, you see there is enough space between two approaching cars to fit your vehicle. You are accelerating as the space approaches, matching your speed to that of the approaching space. As you approach 70 mph, the rest of the cars seem to slow down. Once you are going the same speed as everyone around you, there is no speed. You merge easily into the space, which now has no visible speed.

You probably do this every day but you don't ever think, "Okay, in order to get in there, I have to be exactly 10 feet in front of the rear car and eight feet behind the front car." You also don't try to speed up to 100 mph, hit the brakes, merge into a spot at 60 and then accelerate to 70 before you get smashed in the rear. You definitely don't look at the hood of your own car to gauge how far behind the other car you are. No, unless you're from California, you merge smoothly into a break in traffic by accelerating until you've matched speed with the rest of the vehicles. How far in front of the next car do you have to be so you don't get back-doored? Far enough. It isn't an exact science, you feel your way — it's subconscious.

This is how we ask our students to think about the move to the target in clay sports. Think of merging the gun with the target as you would merge your car with an open space in traffic. When the gun merges in front of the target and is going the same speed as the target, just like the car on the freeway, your move has robbed the target of its speed and you are now controlling the target as you mount and take the shot. If, however, you mount the gun and then try to speed up to get far enough in front of the target to break it, the target is in control of you. This is like trying to merge with 70 mph traffic from a dead stop at the end of the onramp. It will appear faster than it really is.

Control the target from in front. If the gun is not ahead of the bird when the shot is taken, regardless of gun speed, you have no hope of hitting the target. But if the gun is ahead of the target, and even if it is in the "perfect spot," you will miss if the gun speed is too fast or too slow. The nearer the gun speed equals the target speed, the more forgiving the lead and timing are.

For example, let's say we are shooting a 25-yard crossing target and the correct lead is four feet in front. If the gun speed is greater than the target speed, even though the lead is correct when you pull the trigger, chances are you will miss in front. If the gun speed is less than the target speed, even though the lead is correct, chances are you will miss behind when you pull the trigger. The only time the correct lead is correct is when the gun mirrors the target's speed and line.

For those of you with shooting experience, maybe you've experienced this phenomenon and didn't realize it. Have you ever been shooting a pair of easy floating crossers and only hit seven of 10, but you knew the lead was perfect on all 10 of them? What happened on the three you missed? Chances are good that you became more aware of the sight picture than the bird, the gun slowed down, and even with the correct lead, you ended up behind. The correct lead is only correct when the gun and the bird are going the same speed.

Lord help you if you subscribe to the theory of trying to obtain lead via greater gun speed than bird speed. You know, the old mount and slash. This technique has more problems than a Jerry Springer episode, but we have seen shooters who insist on

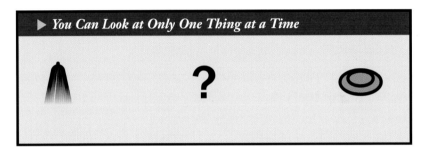

▶ *You Can Look at Only One Thing at a Time*

Your focal vision can focus on only one thing at a time. This illustration will explain it to you:
1. Focus on the muzzle
2. Focus on the target
3. Focus on both of them at the same time.

4. What are you looking at?

When you are looking at the lead, your focal vision is not on either the target or the gun. It is actually in the middle of the two objects. Without focus on the target, the gun will stop and you'll miss behind.

staying with this method — on slashing the gun out in front of the bird at three times the speed of light. When their timing permits, they can have pretty good scores. However, they consistently miss the slow, easy floater ... in front. If they only understood how much slower the targets would appear and how much more forgiving the timing and lead would be if they would just slow down on all shots. They say, "If it ain't broke, don't fix it." We say, "If it ain't broke, fix it!"

Two things happen when the gun moves faster than the target. First, because your eyes instinctively go to the fastest moving object in your field of vision, they will automatically want to go to the gun because it's moving faster than the target. When this happens, the gun stops and the target is missed. *You cannot look at the muzzle and the target at the same time.* Second, if the gun slashes out to the lead, it spends the last three percent of the total swing in a place where it can break the target. Timing then becomes much more critical to break the target. If it spends the last three percent of the swing in front of the target, then it's spending 97 percent of the swing in a place where it can't possibly break the target!

If the gun starts in front of the target and stays in front as it merges to target speed, when the mount is complete, the shot can be taken. Timing is not nearly as critical this way because the gun spends 80 percent of the swing in the lead! The target is slower, the sight pictures are more consistent, there is less panic, and you are in control of the target.

Ever wonder why those people who are great shots appear to move in slow motion? Ever wonder how they can move the gun so little and still break a 50-yard crosser? It's because they all have come to the same conclusion: When the gun speed equals the target speed, the targets slow down and they are easier to break.

It's no wonder the great shots break more targets than anyone else. Their targets are moving slower!

The Ash Method

Review of the basic points in the Ash Method. It's a simple method for a simple game.

- *Focus on the front of the target.*
- *Start the gun in front of the target.*
- *Stay in front of the target.*
- *Merge at the speed of the target, ahead of the target in the breakpoint, and pull the trigger. The gun never moves faster than the bird.*
- *The move and mount begin when the target is in focus and end when the target is killed in the breakpoint.*
- *The move and mount happen in concert with the bird's movement.*

It's a simple game: focus on the target, put the gun where it's going, and pull the trigger.

"Probably 70 to 75 percent of your shots on most sporting clays courses are going to be quartering shots, because they can be thrown in a smaller area than crossing shots."

CHAPTER 9
Quartering targets

We described a crossing move first because it is the move that seems to cause people the most difficulty. It requires the most gun movement and takes more coordination. The move to quartering targets, however, is also important, because so many targets in sporting clays are quartering targets.

Have you ever wondered how many different angles a range owner can utilize for targets on a sporting clays course? It may seem like hundreds, but it really comes down to only two categories: Crossing and quartering. Targets can only cross or quarter. Probably 70 to 75 percent of your shots on most sporting clays courses are going to be quartering shots, because they can be thrown in a smaller area than crossing shots. These may be quartering in or out — from the right or left, or a teal going straight up — you get the picture. You must consider this and identify whether a target is crossing or quartering when you set up for that target. It can be deceptive.

Making a distinction between them is important because there is no swing on a quartering shot. It is more of a perfect point, what we call a "push move." The same principles of the crossing shot still apply, though. You still need to pick a definite breakpoint and commit to it, and your grip and stance will be the same. You still want to control the target from in front, still want to have total focus on the target and pay no attention at all to precise lead during the shot. For those quartering targets with such an extreme angle that you can't see the leading edge — for example, those moving directly away from you — you will want to focus on the rear edge of the target.

In a quartering shot, lead decreases as target distance increases. Also, target speed decreases with target distance. There is a diminishing angle on quartering birds that visually slows the target speed as well. So the quartering bird is a diminishing lead, diminishing speed bird. This means we've got to have a move that diminishes the speed of the muzzle as it merges with the target. It will not be a wild swing or a quick stab. Instead, the quartering shot is a very simple push move — a smooth, slow push at the target. As seen in our video, "How to Practice and Understanding the Move," here's a description of the quartering move made by Craig Hill:

The trap is to Craig's left, about 20 yards away and just slightly in front of him. It will be coming out under speed, peak at about 15 yards above the ground, and land about 65 yards out, on a line almost directly in front of Craig. Craig's head is turned to the left, and his feet are arranged so he is comfortable and in balance in the breakpoint. He has picked a focal point about 15 yards away from the trap on the flight path, and his chosen breakpoint is about 15 yards farther down the flight path. This means his hold point is splitting this distance and is roughly seven and a half yards from both the breakpoint and focal point. (Remember the rule of halves?) His body and eyes are still when he calls "pull."

The target comes out quickly and Craig's initial move on this target is faster than the slow lateral movement on a crossing bird. His head and hands pick up the target quickly, and the first move his hands make is still a lateral move from left to right, toward the breakpoint. His hands are working together, moving up, to the right and pushing out to the breakpoint at the same time, and his eyes are focused on the front edge of the target. The speed of his move diminishes as the target closes in on his breakpoint, and there is virtually no twisting of his shoulders or torso; everything is done with his hands and arms. At the end of his move, it is almost all slow push toward the target as the stock of the gun settles into his face and shoulder simultaneously. As the gun touches his face, the muzzle merges with the target at the breakpoint and he pulls the trigger. You guessed it, Bubba — powder.

Observing this move from the side, it will appear that all Craig did was bring the gun up to his face, point at the target and shoot, and this is almost right. The crossing move was a swing, while the quartering move is a push. The tip of the muzzle traveled close to two feet laterally on the crossing shot. During the quartering move, the tip of the muzzle only moved about 10 inches from left to right. Careful observation, though, will show that there was some lateral movement at the beginning of the quartering move. In fact, Craig's hands moved laterally first, toward the breakpoint and then up. He did not bring the gun up to his shoulder and then swing it along the flight path, chasing the bird. He still never let the bird get in front of him. So there was not as much lateral movement in the quartering move as in the crossing, but the gun still moved laterally before it came up. No matter what move you're making, if the muzzle's first move is up, you're destined to be behind the bird. The only time the first move of the gun should be up is on a target going up or coming in toward the shooter such as a teal or high incomer. Even then, the method of merging with the target applies, but we will get more in-depth on teals later.

As you pictured yourself or Craig making each of the moves, you should have pictured his head and hands moving a little faster at the beginning of the quartering shot than the crosser. His body moved more on the crossing shot, but it also moved slower because it matched the tempo of the target. Of course, you won't have to picture the move in your mind if you get the video, "How to Practice and Understanding the Move," where we offer a bird's-eye view of this move.

This brings up another good point. Your body tempo during the move should mirror the visual speed of the target as you pick it up. For example, on the crossing target, because the trap was farther away, the visual tempo of the target went like this: Slow … slower (as it peaked), and then picking up a little speed as gravity took over and pulled it toward the ground. This means Craig's tempo in the move was: Slow as he picked up the target … slower as he made the initial move with his hands … and then picking up speed as he finished the move and merged gun speed to target speed.

On the quartering bird, the trap was set close to Craig, and the bird came out under more power but diminished in speed and angle as it moved away from him. This means the visual tempo of the target was: fast as the target came out of the trap … slow as the distance increased and it stopped rising … and then even slower as the angle diminished further, heading nearly straight away from Craig. And, of course, the tempo of Craig's move matched this visual speed. Fast (mostly his head) … slow … slower. The importance of the move tempo matching target tempo will not truly be revealed until you begin shooting pairs.

One last thing on the quartering target: Although this is usually an easier target for beginning shooters, it still requires *hard* focus. Remember to focus on a specific part of the bird as well, in most cases on the front of the bird. This way you will not out-swing the quartering bird and shoot past it, which is the most frequent reason for a miss. If you focus on the whole target, your focus will go to the back of the target, causing a miss over or behind. Any excess movement of the gun on any shot will make a big difference.

A lot of advanced shooters can have problems with the quartering move because it is such a simple move and they get used to shooting targets with a lot of excess movement.

So remember to keep the quartering move simple. Focus on the leading edge and make a perfect point with the gun to the target, not a swing. When you get there, pull the trigger. Trust your point. If you hesitate, the information you have given your brain will be different and you will miss the target. Your point is always correct if you are focusing on the front of the target.

Those of you who have children or pets know how to point. Think about how you find a specific place to look, and then you point at it. There is no doubt about what you are pointing at — you know it and so do they. It's always perfect and exactly where you want it to be. Let it work for you here.

*"We can't stress enough
how critical it is to develop a quality move and mount,
and the flashlight drill in this chapter is designed for
this purpose."*

CHAPTER   10
The OSP Flashlight Drill

*For those who would like a visual demonstration of this drill, we cover
it in depth in both our "How to Practice and Understanding the Move"
and "14 Tips to Better Shotgunning" videos.*

Yes, we are going to dedicate an entire chapter to a move and
mount exercise. It's that important. In fact, we should probably
use two chapters. If you've ever seen the movie Karate Kid, you'll
remember how the old man made his student wash cars and paint
fences over and over just to train his muscles to make
the fundamental defensive moves before he ever showed him
the actual moves. Well, this exercise is our version of "wax on,
wax off."

If you really want to go at this the most efficient and least
expensive way, you must train your muscles to make a quality
move and mount before you ever step into a sporting clays stand
or take a lesson. This way the action is subconscious and you

won't spend as much time in the stand fiddling with your move. If you're at a lesson, you'll be wasting valuable learning time because your mind will still be occupied with whether or not you're making the right move. We can't stress enough how critical it is to develop a quality move and mount, and the flashlight drill in this chapter is designed for this purpose. If you'll do this seven days in a row, maybe 20 minutes each day or 50 times each night, you will develop a quality move and mount, and thinking about the gun mount during a shot shouldn't be a problem.

You can practice both the crossing and quartering moves with this exercise. First, get a small flashlight, such as an inexpensive Mini MagLite®, if you don't already have one. If you have a 12-gauge shotgun, get one that takes AA batteries; if you have a

20-gauge, get one that takes AAA. Wrap the handle of the flashlight in tape so it fits snug in the barrel. Have an open choke in the barrel of the shotgun, and for God's sake, *do not* use a loaded gun. Make sure the chamber is empty. The Mini MagLite® flashlight is the kind that allows you to focus the beam of light, so train it down to the smallest diameter circle. Insert the flashlight into the barrel (top barrel if you shoot an over/under).

Wrap clear tape around the barrel of the flashlight so it will fit snugly into the barrel of your shotgun. Insert the flashlight into your unloaded shotgun. Use the top barrel if you shoot an over/under. An open choke works best, skeet or improved cylinder.

To practice the crossing move:

In a room that is dark enough so you can clearly see the beam of your flashlight, but not so dark that you can't see anything else, find the seam where the wall meets the ceiling. Stand in front of it and make sure you have at least five feet clearance on either side of you. Hold the gun in your normal ready position, but make sure the beam of the flashlight is on that seam between the wall and the ceiling. Now, imagine that the seam is the flight path of a crossing target and begin to make your move and mount, keeping the beam of the flashlight on the seam the entire time. You will probably notice that it is shaky at first, dipping under and over the seam as you move, but after practicing you should be able to keep it on the seam throughout the move. Make the move from right to left and then from left to right. Note: Do not mount the gun to your face first (moving it vertically) and then swing the barrel from left to right along the seam.

With our method, the mount is made during the swing, not before, and it ends when the gun touches your face and you pull the trigger. Your first move should be a lateral, or horizontal, move with your pointer hand (the front hand, on the forend of the gun), and at the same time begin mounting the gun with your back hand. The move and mount begin simultaneously. You should make the move and mount in slow motion at first because your goal is to move the light smoothly along the seam, and because muscle memory is programmed with slow, repetitive movements. It doesn't have to be fast, but it must be perfect. As you improve in smoothness, you can begin making the move faster, imagining targets of different speeds, although you shouldn't sacrifice a clean run along the seam for speed. One last reminder: Don't move your head down to the gun. Move the gun up to your face. Your head should have little to no vertical motion during the move.

To practice the left-to-right move:
1. Focus the light to its smallest beam.
2. Stand 8-15 feet away from a wall in a dimly lit room.
3. With the gun in the ready position, point the light in the corner of the room.

4. Move and mount the gun to your face and shoulder following the seam where the wall meets the ceiling with the light.
5. Keep the light on the seam during the move and mount.
6. Don't mount and swing. Move laterally with the light and mount while moving.

7. It helps to have a break-point! (a place on the seam where you are going to finish the mount).
8. The light should move in a straight line and at a constant speed — SLOW!
9. Right-handers — great way to practice your reciprocal move! Left-handers — your hands both go the same direction on this move.

IF IT AIN'T BROKE, FIX IT!

To practice the right-to-left move:

1. Focus the light to its smallest beam.
2. Stand 8-15 feet away from a wall in a dimly lit room.
3. With the gun in the ready position, point the light in the corner of the room.

4. Move and mount the gun to your face and shoulder following the seam where the wall meets the ceiling with the light.
5. Keep the light on the seam during the move and mount.
6. Don't mount and swing. Move laterally with the light and mount while moving.

7. It helps to have a break-point! (a place on the seam where you are going to finish the mount).
8. The light should move in a straight line and at a constant speed — SLOW!
9. Right-handers — your hands both go the same direction on this move. Left-handers — great way to practice your reciprocal move!

To practice the quartering move:

Turn to a corner of the room with the flashlight still in the barrel. Assume your normal stance and point the light at the corner where both walls and the ceiling meet. Keep the circle of light there, and as you make your normal quartering push move, do not let the light move out of that corner. It should not totter left to right or up and down. Keep the light in the corner while you are pushing the gun toward it, mounting the gun to your face. This is sometimes a little easier than the crossing move, but you should still practice it until it is subconscious.

If you want to practice the quartering move at a different angle, for example, imagining a target that is closer to the ground, you can focus on something small in the room or on the walls, say a light switch or the corner of a picture. Train the light on what you've focused on, bring the gun up smoothly in a quartering move, and make sure the light shines on what you are looking at throughout the mount. The front and back hands should work together, keeping the light still as you mount the gun to your face. Even with these exercises, you should not look at the barrel of the gun. Keep your visual focus on the light; it will tell you if the barrel is not moving correctly. In the beginning it's okay to be keenly aware of what your body is doing. The goal is to make the move subconscious. This will take some conscious effort at first, but stay away, at all costs, from making a habit of looking at the barrel.

Most people think that a new student with no bad habits would be easier to teach, but give us someone with a good gun mount and we can get them farther along in a shorter time. We can always refine a gun mount that may not be the best, but if you have no gun mount at all, a lot of time must be spent on learning how to make that right move.

A beginner in a lesson must think not only of all the good

To practice the quartering move:

1. Focus the light to its smallest beam.
2. Stand 8-15 feet away from the corner of a dimly lit room.
3. With the gun in the ready position, point the light into the corner of the room where the walls meet the ceiling.

4. Mount the gun to your face and shoulder without letting the light come out of the corner.

5. Remember to push as you mount the gun. We are practicing the quartering move!

information he/she has received, but also about making a good mount, so as not to get hurt. Conscious thought about making a good gun mount competes with focus on the target. You must be fully focused on that target; 100 percent of your conscious thought must be on killing that bird.

So, if you do these exercises 50 times every night, or 20 minutes a day for seven or eight days, you will see a dramatic increase in the quality of your move. Even for those who are thinking about taking a lesson, if you will do this exercise before your shooting class, you will get more out of the class and won't have to worry as much about the mount because you will have practiced it.

You'll get tired. It's okay. Sit down and take a break if you can't make it to 50 all at once. And you may want to close the blinds or all the neighbors will think you've gone crazy, but when you see the results you probably won't care.

If you swear you've done the flashlight exercise for a week and have a quality move and mount, we're finally ready to talk about lead.

> *"With the zone system there are only three leads: A little bit — some — and a lot."*

CHAPTER 11
Zones

Ever heard the saying, "Close only counts in horseshoes and hand grenades?" Well, it counts in shotgun sports too. Sporting clays is not a game of *exactly*. Neither are trap and skeet for that matter. This fact is one of the big reasons why we want our students to be precise in focus and sloppy in lead. In shotgun sports you are throwing 300 to 500 pellets at the target; you don't need to have the precision of a rifle shooter. When you simply start the gun ahead of the bird, keep the gun ahead of the bird, and move in concert with the bird, then lead becomes very forgiving.

So with the majority of our students, especially beginners, lead is something we don't talk a lot about. Why? Because the first thing our students do when we talk about lead is look at the gun while they're shooting. They want to see how big the lead is. Obviously, because our method is based on focusing only on the front of the target and never on the gun, this is counterproductive. Drill the move and mount first, drill precise focus, and then train your mind to think about lead at one time and one time only. ***Before you address the target.*** We have a system that makes perceived lead very easy. With our system you will never think about lead while you are shooting, only while you are carrying out your pre-shot routine. You will think briefly about lead when you are analyzing the flight path of the target you are about to shoot, and then you will not consciously think about lead until your pre-shot routine on the next shot or station.

Over years of instruction, we've found that our students have a much easier time inserting the gun where it needs to be when they think of lead in terms of windows, in general terms rather than specifically.

In fact, we have a descriptive word for it — slather. We tell our students, "Just slather it out in front of the bird."

"But how far?" they'll ask.

Well, here's something that will make it really simple. It's called the OSP Zone System. With the zone system there are only three leads: a little bit — some — and a lot. Or as the Bubbas down in Lafayette, Louisiana would call it: OD, WOD, and WWOD. That's "out dare," "way out dare," and "way, way out dare." Here's how the zones break down.

Zone One   *"Out dare" — Mark Landry*

If you want to be technical, zone one is anywhere from the front edge of the target to two feet out. We don't say the lead is two feet, we say insert the gun anywhere between the front edge of the target and two feet out. You want to give yourself a mental picture of this, so it might be a good idea to take a box or a two-foot circle and see how it looks from different distances — 10 yards, 20 yards, 30 yards away. The subconscious mind remembers pictures much better than it calculates measurement, so when you think zone one, you'll remember the picture.

When do you use zone one? Any time the lead is right at the front of the target, or just in front of it. Zone one targets are incomers and slow crossing and quartering birds; in fact, most quartering targets take zone one lead. So when you are preparing to shoot a slow crossing or quartering target, you can tell yourself, "This is a zone one target," before you address the target and call "pull." Then during the shot you don't have to measure it by looking at the gun. You can just insert the muzzles into zone one as you make the mount and take the shot.

Zone Two   *"Way out dare" — Mark Cruse*

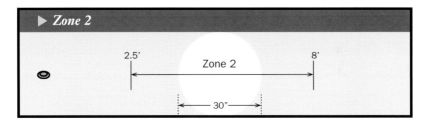

A zone two lead is about two and a half to eight feet in front of the bird. This might appear to be too big a window, but we promise you that if you use this general window on the proper target, it will work. When you see a target that is fast or one that is far away and fast, if you tell yourself, "Okay, that's a zone two picture," you can insert on the bird into zone two without conscious effort during the shot. You must tell yourself to put it into zone two before you address the shot, because if you don't, you'll put it in zone one. That's because 70 to 80 percent of targets on a sporting clays course are zone one targets. Be sloppy with lead and precise in focus.

If you're still worried about how your subconscious will make the right correction given such a large lead window, we'll try to calm your fears with this little thought experiment. Think about the size of a normal shot cloud at a distance between 20 and 35 yards. In this range, it's going to have a diameter of about 30 inches. Now picture this 30-inch diameter as a ball and place that ball in your zone two picture, from two and a half to eight feet. This ball already covers from two and a half to almost five feet out. To get the outer edge of the ball to touch that eight-foot boundary, it doesn't have to roll very far, does it? Now the window doesn't look so big with a 30-inch ball inside of it. This just shows you that it will take very little gun movement to adjust your shot cloud from one end of zone two to the other, providing you use the right choke.

What kinds of targets are zone two targets? Close crossers that are fast! Medium distance crossers at medium speed; long crossers that are slow; any crossing target at 30-plus yards, including chandels; rabbits rolling beyond 35 yards; flying rabbits beyond 25 yards; and dropping teal at 40 to 45 yards.

Zone Three   _"Way, way out dare." — Doss Bourgeois_

How much lead does a zone three picture take? A bunch. This is a zone that runs anywhere from eight feet out to infinity.

You won't see many of these, you won't see many at all, and this is why we're not going to elaborate too much on them, especially in a book only intending to cover the basics of shotgun sports. It's enough to say that to make a target into a zone three picture, it is going to take so much speed or so much distance (or both) that you will probably recognize it right away.

After reading about the zones, you still might be saying, "No way, that's too vague, it won't work." Well, believe us, it does work.

It works because your subconscious has the ability to make a minor correction at the end of every shot to make the lead perfect and on line every time, as long as you are consciously focused on

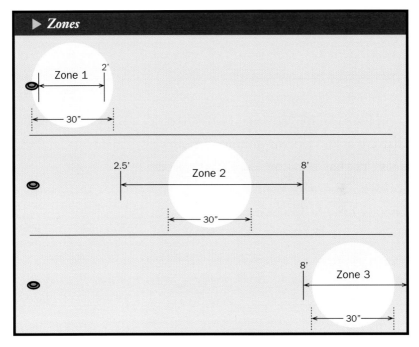

Looking at the three zones together, you can see with a 30" circle overlaid on each that it takes very little correction to cover each of the three zones. You can also see why we refer to lead as a little bit, some, and a lot. The key to the zone system is: When the insertion of the gun is into the correct zone, the subcon- scious can make a minor correction, if needed, before the shot is taken. This decreases muzzle awareness dramati- cally. If a lead change is necessary, either double it or cut it in half. Small lead changes are insignificant because of the size of the shot cloud.

the front of the target and not on the lead and as long as you insert the gun somewhere in the correct zone. The key phrase here: minor correction. As long as you are in the ballpark, the subconscious will do its job. Another big key is for you to trust your subconscious enough to put lead into its care. In your pre-shot routine, once you have classified a shot as a zone one, two or three lead picture, think no more about it. Let your body do the rest.

If you still feel confused about what the zone pictures look like after reading all this, we would like to again shamelessly plug our video, "How to Practice and Understanding the Move." In it, Gil gives a very hands-on presentation of the zone system and what each zone looks like.

To get a feeling for the zones on your own, find a simple crossing bird. Shoot it where you know you're putting the gun in zone one, maybe about 15 to 20 yards out. Keep putting it in zone one. Then start backing up, a little at a time, until you get to the point where you know, "Okay, I'm in zone two now." You'll begin to understand what zone two pictures look like.

Creating Lead

As you get a handle on the zone system, it is important to understand what creates lead on a moving target. Only two things create lead: speed and distance. Of the two, speed creates more lead than distance. If a target is fast, it's going to take lead. Think about this as you analyze targets. Eventually you will get a feel for how fast a target must be moving to put it into zone two category lead. When you see this you will understand how rare zone three targets are. For a target to be zone three, it will have to be a long way off, and traveling at a high rate of speed, or at mid-range and traveling close to the speed of sound. Speed creates lead. So, fast target, fast hands ... slow target, slow hands.

But let us tell you something here: Be really careful about this. Stay in zone one until you get your move down. If there is not enough consistency in your move to keep your gun moving 90 to 95 percent the same speed as the target, what good does it do to program pictures? None, because it doesn't matter how accurate your zone picture is if you're moving the gun faster or slower than the target. Programming pictures is done *after* the move is programmed in the subconscious database.

One more thing — you can be aware that the gun is out in front of the bird. It's okay. A lot of people have trouble because in trying not to have any awareness of the gun, they try too hard and end up losing focus on the target. There will be some peripheral awareness of the gun, and that's okay, just don't focus on the gun. If you're over five percent aware of where the gun is, you're looking at the gun. Ninety-six to 100 percent of your focus must be on the target. The more you know about where your gun is, the more you're looking at it, and the harder it is to hit targets.

Remember what kind of instrument you have in your hands. A shotgun is a scattergun; it's not a laser-guided missile. It's not meant to be aimed; it's meant to be pointed. It's meant to be slathered. Precision lead is not important when you are shooting 300 to 500 pellets that spread into a 30-inch diameter cloud. Say it with us one more time: ***Be sloppy in lead, precise in focus.***

“You will never shoot better than the quality of your basic move and mount.”

CHAPTER   12
The constant

The biggest difference between the games of skeet and trap and the game of sporting clays is the constant. They all involve shooting clay targets thrown from a trap, they all involve the same basic skill set, and they're all a hell of a lot of fun to play. But in skeet and trap, the targets are the constant. In sporting clays, your move must be the constant.

Trap is a clays game where standard targets are all thrown from one house at least 16 yards in front of the shooter. There are five shooting positions/stations running in a slightly curved line from left to right behind the trap, with the third station directly behind the trap. Targets are thrown one at a time, and all the targets are quartering (within a horizontal angle of 44 degrees), but the shooter never knows at which angle the target will be thrown.

In skeet there are two trap houses, one high house on the left and a low house on the right. There are eight shooting positions/stations arranged in a semi-circle, with the first station at the far left edge of the circle under the high house, and the seventh station at the far right edge next to the low house. Station eight is midway between and on line with stations one and seven. As shooters move from station to station, they are presented with different looks at each target, from quartering to crossing trajectories, but they always know which house the targets will be coming from, and the flight paths are always the same. Two single targets are shot from each of the eight stations and pairs are thrown (two targets at the same time) at four stations.

Sporting clays is often called "golf with a shotgun," and the description is not far off. It's a game created to mimic game birds (or rabbits) and their flight patterns, and the stations (usually called stands) are set up in courses. Most courses have 10 to 15 stands from which a total of 100 birds will be thrown. The target presentations in sporting clays vary wildly, from tower shots, to low streaking outgoers, to rolling rabbits, to long curling incomers, to springing teal that rise straight up and fall straight down. The key word is *variety*. The targets are typically thrown in two types of pairs, true pairs and report pairs, with an occasional following pair. True pairs are individual targets thrown at the same time; in a report pair, as soon as the shooter pulls the trigger on the first target, the second target is thrown. A following pair consists of two single targets thrown from the same trap, with the second thrown as soon as the machine can cock and throw it. The shooter calls "pull" once, and the birds are thrown one right after another.

As if it weren't enough to have endless speeds, distances, angles, target combinations, and natural landscape features to play with, the game of sporting clays has specialty targets that vary in size and flight characteristics, just to keep you on your toes. As the level of competition increases, so does the number of variables to make it more challenging. It's a fun game to play

Gil's Guide to Gun Speed and Visual Speed

Have you ever wondered when you are watching other people shoot a station why the targets appear so slow? Yet when you step into the box they seem to speed up? Why do you think this happens? Well, let's think about the nature of speed. Speed is a relationship between two objects. The target's visual speed is equal to the difference between the gun speed and the target speed. If the gun speed is equal to the target speed, the bird will appear to slow down and float regardless of how fast it is actually going. If, on the other hand, the gun speed is greater than the target speed, the target will appear to speed up and become erratic in flight.

Why does the visual speed of the target decrease as you move the gun in tempo with the target? This is the stuff of Einstein, man. It's what the physicists and engineers of the world call relative velocity. We call it visual speed.

*Let's just say you and I are standing beside the freeway, and all the cars are going 70 mph. They would be whizzing by, right? Now someone stops, picks us up, and we start going 70 mph with the rest of the cars. Everything appears to slow down. Even though we are going 70 mph, the cars that were whizzing by us now appear to be still because we are all going the same direction and the same speed. **You can do this to the target.** When the muzzle and the target are going the same speed and in the same direction (just like the cars) everything appears to slow down. This is why the targets look real slow when you're watching your buddy shoot, then seem to speed up when you step into the stand. This is because you're moving your gun too fast; you're not in sync with the bird. Don't always blame your misses on lead. The only time the right lead is the right lead in a consistent way is when the gun is going the same speed as the bird.*

but a difficult, if not impossible, game to master, and that's what keeps people coming back.

From here on out we will be concentrating on the game of sporting clays. The same fundamentals apply to all clays games, whether it's sporting, trap or skeet, but our specialty is sporting clays. Plus, it is basically an elaboration of the games of skeet and trap, so even if trap and skeet are your games of choice, we think you'll be able to get a lot of helpful information from the following chapters.

It's important to remember in sporting clays the only constant is your move. In trap and skeet, the targets are the constant. The target presentations are the same worldwide. In a game with as many variables as sporting clays, something has to become a constant. The consistency and quality of your move and mount must become the constant. The better and more consistent your move and mount become, the slower the targets appear to fly and the easier they become to break consistently.

Bird Hunters Coming to Clay Sports

An introduction to clay sports can be humbling for even the best bird hunters. You might fancy yourself an expert hunter — you may have been doing it since the days of black powder. But if you go barreling onto a clays range for the first time thinking you're gonna bust every target, you could be in for some frustration.

Usually we see bird hunters come to the clays range thinking they will just tune up a little for the hunt. Those who don't understand the fundamental difference between shooting live birds and shooting clay targets hardly ever do well. They'll go to a clays range thinking they're going to own it, but after hitting six birds out of 25 on a round of skeet, they can hear their name being announced over a loudspeaker as the leading candidate for the Clay Pigeon Preservation Society Award. Excitement turns to utter despair.

It's a damn shame if they walk away frustrated and decide to swear off clay sports altogether, because all they need to do to fix the problem is understand why they are missing.

Bird hunters crash and burn on the clays course because their eyes do not maintain focus on the clay target. Remember when we told you the eyes automatically go to the fastest object in your field of vision? (Chapter 8: pg 47) Well, it's easier to focus on a live bird because their wings will always be moving faster than anything else in the picture. This gives hunters something to focus on, something that will easily hold their focus. In addition, this allows for the hunters to get away with some slop in their gun mount (excessive speed) without sacrificing focus on the bird. They also have a head to look at on a live bird. Their eyes can then move to the head of the bird and they will put the barrel where it's going. A lot of hunters and shooters don't realize that if they do not look at the head (or the leading edge of the target) their eyes will naturally go to the back of the bird. If they are looking at the back, and the gun goes where the eyes are focused, then the gun will go to the back of the bird. How many times have you seen tail feathers come off a bird? Make your eyes go to the head of the bird, and the gun will follow. The same principle applies in clay sports, although usually hunters have to make a conscious effort to focus on the leading edge of the target because they don't have those beating wings to grab their focus. And because they have no beating wings to hold their focus, if the move and mount are the least bit fast or irregular, the shooter will lose focus on the target and see the gun.

Here's another question bird hunters have when they come out to a lesson: Why, if I miss with the first shot, do I usually hit with a second or third? It's our experience that you missed the first shot because you were looking at the lead, but when you realized you missed you simply looked at the bird and instinctively shot at it, hitting it with the second or third shot. Another reason birds are missed on the first shot is because the gun doesn't always get to your face. When the first shot is missed, you then get the gun up to your face and are able to hit the bird. You don't have to knock yourself unconscious or bring the gun up at light speed, but it's important that it comes all the way to your face.

The best thing you can do to help your bird hunting and clay shooting? Practice your gun mounts before you go. We cannot tell you how many hunters we see who have bruises up and down their arms because of improper gun mounts. They come to our clinics and ask why they hurt so much, and it's always because the guns are getting to their shoulders improperly.

The cheek is the anchor point for the mount. If the gun is mounted to the cheek, it will always be on your shoulder. If you try to mount the gun to your shoulder first, more often than not it will end up on your arm. Last time we looked, the shoulder was closer to the collarbone than the elbow. Get that gun out and practice with it before you go on your hunts. It will make for a more enjoyable time and a more successful hunt.

And if you're a hunter new to clay sports, remember to maintain hard focus on the front edge of the target. Also, be aware that if you're swinging the muzzles faster than the target is moving, your eyes will go to the gun and you will likely miss. We say "likely" because even a blind pig finds an acorn once in a while.

IF IT AIN'T BROKE, FIX IT!

> **"** *The beauty (and the bitch) of sporting clays is found in all the different things the targets do and all the different environments they do them in.* **"**

CHAPTER 13
Sporting clays target presentations

We've told you in Chapter 9 that sporting clays targets can only do two things: cross or quarter. Well, we didn't lie, but that's only the beginning. The thing is, even within the parameters of crossing and quartering, sporting clays targets can still be thrown in an endless variety of different presentations. And that's just when they're throwing one at a time.

The beauty (and the bitch) of sporting clays is found in all the different things the targets do and all the different environments they do them in. They're springing straight up in tree cover, rolling along the ground, moving fast, moving slow, coming out of a 100-foot tower or buzzing along just a few feet above the ground. They're arcing, curling, and disappearing behind hills and bushes — you get the picture. Flight paths are like snowflakes; no two are the same, even if the targets are coming out of the same trap. They might be similar, but they won't ever be exactly the same. This is why focus and solid fundamentals are so important. If you break a pair at a stand and decide you're going to match exactly what you did on the next pair, even if you are able to do that, you could miss the target because it might not do the same thing as the first. You have to feel and react to each target in each pair, not your memory of the first. React, don't duplicate!

So focus and fundamentals will carry you a long way in sporting clays, but for each presentation there are shooting tips that will get you just a little bit further. You learn these bits of insight through experience, but we've found that dispensing our tips for each target presentation helps shooters absorb them faster.

That said, we don't have the space or the inclination to go through every target presentation we've seen and what we've learned from it. We want to concentrate on the fundamentals in this book, and many of you can't handle all that we know just yet. Our students laugh when we tell them this, but it's true. Don't get on a bull if the pony can buck you off.

Let's start with the pony then, the basic trajectories you will see in sporting clays, the first trajectories you should master. They are: crossing (both left-to-right and right-to-left), quartering (both left-to-right and right-to-left), targets going up and targets coming down. For the following discussion, we'll assume everyone is right-handed. If you're left-handed, just imagine all the left-to-right tips are really right-to-left and vice versa. (Wherever you see the word "left" substitute the word "right", and insert "left" when you see "right")

Left-To-Right Crossers
Big Tip: don't move your hands in the same direction on this trajectory. The hands must move in opposite directions to be consistent and successful.

A right-handed shooter has an
unobstructed view of all targets
coming from her left because
the target is on what we call
the "two-eyed" side of the gun.

The left-to-right crossing trajectory is the easiest to see because the shooter doesn't have to look across the muzzles to see the target, but it's also the most difficult move. This is because the hands are working against each other, doing opposite things in opposite directions at the same time. The left hand is moving palm-forward to the right, and the right hand is moving palm-inward to the left and up to the face; it's what we call a reciprocal move.

Let us repeat: The front hand must push the muzzles to the right and, at the same time, the back hand must push the stock left and up to the face. Both hands must move together to bring the gun to the face without a seesaw effect. Since the hands are doing two different things, they don't always work together. You must practice this to make it smooth. The best practice is the OSP Flashlight Drill (Chapter 10) and station six on a skeet

In the left-to-right move the hands must move in opposite directions (right-handed shooters).

The front hand is pushing the muzzles right to the breakpoint, the back hand is pushing the butt stock to the left into Gil's face and shoulder.

We call this a reciprocal move. It is the hardest move to program for a right-handed shooter and must be practiced a lot.

IF IT AIN'T BROKE, FIX IT!

range, where you can shoot the targets from the left, or high house. (See our video, "How to Practice and Understanding the Move," as a reference.) Make sure your mount is perfect, then start backing up the distance. Start close until you feel your move is right, then start moving back, striving for consistency in feel, rhythm, and timing.

As you make the move, keep in mind barrel speed and target speed must be the same so you can keep focus on the target. Your eyes go to the fastest moving thing in the picture, and if the gun is moving too fast your eyes will go to it.

The key to this reciprocal move is pushing with that front hand and moving the back hand in the opposite direction up toward the face. Don't let the back hand go to the right with the front hand and try to bring your face down to it. We recommend you practice this move three times more than the right-to-left.

Right-To-Left Crossers
Big Tip: learn the soft, easy "J" move.

In general, the right-to-left crossing move is a much easier move to make than the left-to-right because both hands are working together, moving in the same direction. Don't let this get you all smug, though, or you might end up missing this trajectory time after time, saying bad things about your momma and blaming all of it on an eye dominance problem. This trajectory is actually harder for most people because you must look across the muzzles to see the bird, so the difficulty of this presentation is in seeing the target. Right-to-left targets have a tendency to lose you by disappearing behind the barrel of the gun. This will really be apparent if you're mounting early and chasing the lead.

Here's our solution to this problem: the soft, easy "J" move. On any right-to-left picture (vice versa for lefties) you want to

The right-to-left target (right-handed shooter) has the greatest amount of visual confusion. This is because the shooter must focus on the target while looking across the gun.

hold your gun just a little lower and a little farther out, toward the breakpoint. Then, as you mount the gun, insert the muzzles from underneath in front of the bird in a soft move that traces the reversed shape of the letter "J." It doesn't have to be really exaggerated, just enough to keep the gun under the target's flight line. If you don't do this, the bird will pull your eyes to the gun and off the line of its flight.

Our good friend "gotch-eyed" Ron at Camanche Hills Sporting Clays in California was having so much trouble with right-to-left crossers that he thought he'd developed an eye dominance problem. He was sure of it, man, because he just wasn't hitting them like he used to. Gil took him out to have a look and sure enough, 20 minutes later Ron was making the soft, easy "J" move and hitting every right-to-left crosser out of the trap. His eyes were fine, but he wasn't giving them a chance to

In the right-to-left move both hands are moving in the same direction.

The front hand is pulling the muzzles left to the breakpoint. The back hand is pushing the butt stock left into Gil's face and shoulder.

A fairly easy move to master for a right-handed shooter.

see the target because the gun was blocking the view. He was starting with the gun on the flight line, not below, and in close to the trap instead of out away from the trap.

Quartering Targets: from the left and right
Big Tip: Let the front hand do most of the work by "pushing" out to the breakpoint.

We're going to save a tree and point you back to Chapter 9. Most of the tips you need for left and right quartering targets will be found there. We'll just say this: Because the quartering move is less complicated than the crossing move, when you miss a quartering bird it is usually because you were not focused hard on the leading edge of the target or you didn't push the gun to the breakpoint. Remember: You push the gun on quartering shots and swing the gun on crossing shots. Focus on that edge and point at it.

Also, the back hand should be nothing more than a guide in this move. The grip pressure should be the same in both hands, but the front hand should do the pointing, while the back hand gently brings the gun to the face. If you get too much back hand, the muzzles will seesaw.

Teal Shots
Big Tip: Don't try to wait until this bird is "still."

Teal shots have two flight trajectories: those going up and those coming down.

The simple definition of a teal target is any target that is thrown straight up, or at any trajectory that's narrower than the McDonald's arches (between 70 and 90 degrees). The teal trajectory is usually a hard shot for a lot of people, especially these days when target setters are coming up with so many ways to present teal.

The move on the teal target is the same push move made on all quartering targets. There must be some vertical movement of the muzzles as you track the flight path. In fact, the lateral move on a teal is up!

Most of the shooters we see try to take the teal at the top of the arch. When we ask them why they do this, it's either because someone else told them to or because they want to shoot the bird when it's still.

Hellooooo? When it's still?

The problem with this is the bird is never still. It moves from rising to falling but it is never still. Yes, this target comes off the trap arm quickly and slows down faster than all other trajectories, and it's moving the slowest at the top of its arch, but we guarantee you will miss it most of the time when you try to wait until it's "still." Why? Well, how do you know when it's "still," or no longer rising? The only time you know that the bird is no longer rising is when it's falling. If you pull the trigger at the top edge of the bird at the top of the arch, when it looks still, you will be shooting above a bird that is already falling.

If you want to hit this bird consistently, shoot it while it's still rising. Or, shoot under it as it begins to fall, but we don't recommend trying the old point-and-shoot like you've got a rifle in your hands, knocking beer cans off a fence.

The teal target is most often missed because the shooter sees the target when he pulls the trigger! Say what? Well, unlike all other targets, because the teal is rising (going up) the gun must be over (above) the target in order to be in front of it. But when the gun is over the target it will then obstruct the view of the target when it is in the correct lead.

Some folks tackle this situation by swinging through a teal target and pulling the trigger as the gun passes through (covers up) the bird. However, we prefer another method. We teach our

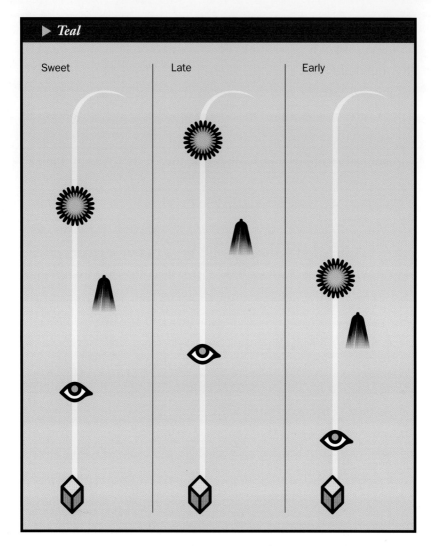

Sweet   Late   Early

The teal is a quartering target going up. When shot sweet or late, the muzzle should be about half-way between the focal point and the breakpoint. The muzzles should be off-line to the right (right-handed shooters) enough so you can see your focal point with both eyes (see targets on the 6 to 12 o'clock line in Chapter 7). It is important that the initial move of the gun is muzzles up to the breakpoint with both hands after you have focused on the target. Insert the muzzles over the target and take the shot. You will find that over is very forgiving. Put it up there and pull the trigger.

When shooting the teal early like the quartering shot, the focal point is critical. You must see it quickly in order to shoot it quickly. The hold point will be much closer to the breakpoint and still just off-line to the right. The initial move of the muzzles must be straight up to the breakpoint. The teal target is typically thrown faster than other targets because it is thrown up against gravity. Because of its speed, when shot early, you must insert the muzzles well over the target to hit it. Don't be afraid. Put it up there and pull the trigger.

students to simply start the muzzles off to the right of the bird's path with a higher hold point. (About the half-way point between the trap and where the bird is peaking). We tell them to have a focal point just above the trap. As the bird exits, we teach them to push the muzzles up, insert the muzzles above the bird, and take the shot.

Muzzle Awareness

Most missed targets in sporting clays can be traced back to too much visual awareness of the gun. Here are a few reasons for muzzle awareness:
- *the gun moves too fast*
- *the gun was mounted too fast or too early*
- *the bird got ahead of the gun and the gun had to catch up*
- *the shooter checked the lead*
- *fluorescent bead sights*
- *a last-second head adjustment*
- *the hold point is too close to the trap*
- *the hold point is over the line of the target*
- *the eyes are moving when the shooter calls "pull."*
- *mechanical thinking*

The confusing thing to most shooters and some coaches is that the result (missing in front or behind) of too much muzzle awareness is the same as the result of cross-dominance! This is why our system of perfecting the quality of the move solves 90 percent of the mysteries surrounding why you missed. This is also why we continue to say (in spite of ridicule) *that the number of people who have a cross-dominance problem is dramatically fewer than the number of people who think they do. It is easier to blame the miss on "intermittent cross-dominance" than the fact that you need to work on your move and mount.*

You also must learn to trust yourself, stop thinking, and focus beyond the gun. The more you consciously know about what the gun is doing and where the gun is, the less you know about where the target is and what it's doing. We're sure Yogi Berra would be able to focus 100 percent on the target and 50 percent on the gun, but he's the only one! This is not a game of swing mechanics and lead. It is, however, a game of focus, rhythm, feel, timing, and trust. Until your move ascends to a level of quality where it not only happens without thought but it's so good that you can actually feel it, you can't even hope to begin the journey of mental performance. Practice your move and mount relentlessly. You will never shoot better than the quality of your basic move and mount.

The Targets of Sporting Clays

It might not hold your interest quite like *The Girls Of Muscle Car Digest*, but getting to know The Targets Of Sporting Clays is important, especially if you want to compete.

The Standard: Miss January

The "girl next door" of shotgun targets, you'll see more standards on a sporting clays range than any other type. The only target not considered a "specialty target," she can be any variety of colors, from all orange, all black, or all white, to orange dome or yellow dome.

Measurements: *4-1/4 inches (108-110 mm) wide*

Favorite Thing To Do: *Everything. There is an almost endless variety of presentations for this target.*

How To Score With Her: *See Chapters 1-11. Like all other targets, she breaks easy when hit on the underside, as will happen when she's crossing directly overhead. Most difficult to break when all she's showing is dome. Hardest to see when all she's showing is edge.*

The Midi: Miss February

You'll miss in more months than February if you mistake the slightly smaller midi for her cousin the standard. She's all orange or all black.

Measurements: *3-1/2 inches (90mm) wide*

Favorite Thing To Do: *She loves to make you think she's a standard at a greater distance, and this also makes her look faster. This illusion will often cause unsuspecting shooters to shoot too far in front. The most aerodynamic of the domed targets, the midi may look like a standard, but she maintains her velocity and flight path longer. She's also harder to break because she's so compact.*

How To Score With Her: *First, make sure what kind of target you're shooting. Ask the trapper to tell you the target type and the order in which they will be thrown. Next, if it's at all possible, shoot the midi later in the flight path after she's shed some of her speed.*

The Mini: Miss March

The smallest of all targets, she's all one color and gets her "aspirin" nickname from her size, but she can also give you headaches if you're not prepared to meet her.

Measurements: *2-3/8 inches (60mm) wide*

Favorite Thing To Do: *The mini leaves the trap faster and slows down faster after coming out of the trap than any other target.*

How To Score With Her: *Don't look to shoot the mini right off the trap. She's too fast for that, so take her after she has shed some speed. She is easy to break because she is so small, and this also makes pellet count more important than pellet size. Shoot 9's or 8-1/2's at Miss March to keep her from slipping through your fingers!*

The Rabbit: Miss April

The rabbit can leave you feeling like quite a thumper, especially if you don't focus on the center circle or if you try to guess where she's going. Her colors are always solid.

Measurements: *4-1/4 inches wide, (same as standard) but the rabbit has a very thick rim that allows her to roll along the ground without breaking. This makes her heavier.*

Favorite Thing To Do: *The rabbit can be thrown in the air, but you'll usually find her mimicking her namesake on the ground. She really likes to make you chase her and anticipate her bounces.*

How To Score With Her: *Instead of focusing on the leading edge (as you would a target in the air), focus on the center of the rabbit. Don't try to anticipate bounces, and remember that the rabbit will come out fast and slow down quickly each time she hits the ground.*

The Battue: Miss May

Thin as a shadow, the battue is the queen of curl and is always either orange or black, but she can be broken with fewer than three pellets.

Measurements: *4-1/4 inches wide, but the battue has no dome.*

Favorite Thing To Do: *After getting out of the trap, the battue loves to curl like a Frisbee thrown upside down. This causes problems, especially if you're not expecting her to do it. Because you want your move to mirror the target, the move on the battue is different than on any other target.*

How To Score With Her: *Miss May is almost always shot when she is in her curl. The typical mistake is to start the move from underneath, moving to her from six o'clock before she starts to curl. If you do this, when she decides to curl, you'll be trapped behind her. So play the battue like an outfielder would play a fly ball, controlling her from well in front, never from underneath. And remember, in front means in front on line. In front of any curling target is never under and in front. In front is always in front, on line with the flight path.*

In either method, the most common mechanical mistake is to move the back hand first, causing the muzzles to move down first. To recover, the shooter has to then slash up and chase the bird. Both hands must move up to break the teal consistently.

Dropping Targets

There are two methods we prefer to deal with dropping targets. The first is what we call "stabilizing the picture." This means you insert the muzzles under the target as it begins to fall, matching the muzzle speed with the target speed. This stabilizes the picture (or lead) because the target does not appear to move when the gun is moving the same speed. Once the picture is stable, you pull the trigger.

A second method for dropping teal targets is one we learned from Roger Silcox of England. Start with a hold point off to the side of the flight path of the dropping target. As the target begins to fall, move the muzzles laterally toward the breakpoint maintaining focus on the target. It is critical that your move is in sync with the accelerating speed of the target. When the target and the muzzles merge together in the breakpoint, take the shot. It is critical that the shot be taken instantaneously when the mount is complete. Like Daniel Olson said, "The gun is on your cheek for a half of a split second and you take the shot." It will feel like you are just shooting right at the target. Reading this, you might think there is high risk to this method, but when practiced, it is easier and more reliable than any other method.

"You are establishing confidence in your game during your practice."

CHAPTER 14
How to practice

Practicing in a dimly lit room with a flashlight will give you a smooth move and mount, but it's not going to help much with target recognition, picking breakpoints, or getting a feel for how your gun behaves when fired. Plus, if you do it too much your spouse might think you need some counseling, and the neighbor kids will start running away from you. To avoid the anti-social tag, to get better at the game, and to start having more fun, you will eventually need to start practicing on an actual clays range.

Not like we ever have to tell people to do this — usually they go overboard and are out on the range as soon as (in many cases, before) they have a decent mount, shooting 100-target courses for score and dreaming of winning the big tournaments. This is not the smartest way to go about practicing. We wouldn't even call this practicing; we'd call it monkeying around. If all you want to do is monkey around on the clays course, competing with your friends for score, that's fine, monkey away. We'd even recommend it, because, hey, it's fun to monkey.

If you're serious about improving, and if you have aspirations of competing, don't monkey around and call it practice. Going out and shooting every target in a course for score will not bring nearly as much improvement as developing a practice routine and working on specific aspects of your game. By the way, we do have a video called "How to Practice and Understanding the Move," which goes into all of this in great detail, providing a good visual reference for the material in this chapter and Chapter 15.

The initial routine we recommend for working on your game goes like this: Go out and shoot singles — one target at a time — at five different stands at your course or from four different places on a skeet field. Don't shoot anything longer than 25 yards away. Find the sweet spot to break the target (Chapter 3, page 17) and break it there 10 times, then move the breakpoint to a different spot and break it there 10 times, then move it again. This will give you three different ways to break a target from one trap. Remember when we told you that you'd have to learn to break it in three different places? (Our video titled "Strategy and How to Play the Game" deals exclusively with this point.)

There should be three main objectives to your practice. One: To make the proper move. Two: To learn how to hit targets in different places. Three: To make a habit of staying focused for 10 targets. You have to do this in a tournament, so why not start practicing it? This should be the order in which you make your priorities. Your focus does no good if you can't make a quality move.

Be very critical with making the right move in practice. Be aware of your body and how the move feels. Did it feel right? Was the mount perfect? Did you finish the shot in balance? Was the focus the best it could be? Did you see the front of the target? Make it perfect. In your practice you are making your mechanics perfect. Once they are perfect, you have to do them over and over again so they become subconscious.

By learning how to hit targets in different places, you will also find yourself becoming more confident in stepping up to a stand you've never shot, because you will know you can hit any target any place. When it's time to hit a target in a different place, you will know you can do it.

Again, don't go to your practice to shoot a score, work on your game. You'll have enough opportunities to embarrass yourself when you start competing, so why would you want to embarrass yourself in practice?

You are establishing confidence in your game during your practice. This will really diminish the number of times you do embarrass yourself. (It's bound to happen at least once, right?) In practice you are removing doubt, overcoming the fear of not hitting these targets, and adding the ability to hit them at any spot you want. As your confidence level rises, so will your scores when you do start competing.

Think about it this way: A professional football team plays an actual game one day a week. They practice the component parts of the game five days a week. These are amazing athletes that have been playing their game at a very high level for years, and they still break their practice up into fundamentals. It's a system that works!

Of all our students, the ones who are really dedicated to practicing this way have excelled the most in their game. Avoid the temptation to go out shooting for score with your friends when you have committed the day to practice. Yes, other people might think you're silly for spending so much time at one stand, but once they see their scores below yours at competition, they'll see that you're silly and good.

"Attitude has more to do with success and failure than any one thing."

CHAPTER 15
What to practice

Just like all the basketball greats who began their rise to stardom by first learning the all-important buzzer lob from half-court, you will embark on a great sporting clays career by shooting true pairs at 50 yards away.

Sound ass-backwards? That's good, because it is, but you would be amazed what some people want to practice when they come to a lesson. Usually in our clinics, when we ask everyone what they want to learn to shoot, they say "hard targets." This translates into long targets for most people because beginning and intermediate shooters most often miss long targets, and the targets we miss are the difficult targets, right? *Not*!

Well, we would be fine in teaching them to shoot the long targets if they could hit everything within 25 to 30 yards. If they don't have a move that's good enough to hit 90 percent of the close ones, then we're going to have big problems with the 50-yard crosser.

Distance compounds errors in technique. If you have poor technique, it won't result in nearly as many misses on close targets as it does on longer ones. You can get by with a sloppy gun mount or a quick, choppy move and still score okay at 25 to 30 yards. But we can't teach you to hit long crossers with a sloppy move and mount, and you can't improve a sloppy move and mount unless you practice close targets. See the predicament in practicing long targets before you can hit the close ones?

So what should you practice?

Practice your crossing move on a skeet field like we talked about in the last chapter, shooting singles 10 times in a row in three different breakpoints. Master everything within 30 yards and make your move subconscious. Don't neglect making your plan before you call "pull" at each station, and don't neglect consciously picking a breakpoint, a focal point, and a hold point. Tell yourself, "I'm going to see it there (at the focal point) and I'm going to break it there (at the breakpoint)." Establish a consistent shooting routine. Your goal is not just to break the bird, but to break the bird in the chosen breakpoint.

Pay special attention to the crossing targets. Master the crossing move, dominate it; shoot crossers on the skeet range until you're sick of them, until there is no thought, until you break them every time. You're developing a database of muscle memory, which is created through slow, repetitive movement. You will need to make somewhere between 2,500 to 3,000 reps to get it in your subconscious database.

When you've mastered the skeet field, practice your quartering move on a trap field. Go to station three. If you can, and it's safe, move closer to the trap. Lock it down so the bird is going straight out from you. Pick out your breakpoint and break the target in three different spots: sweet, late, and early. Once you're comfortable with the move there, shoot the target five to

10 times in a row from each station available, continuing to shoot three different breakpoints. The optimum sequence should be stations three, four, two, five, and one. Own each trajectory. Shoot each trajectory sweet, late, and early. Shoot it five to 10 times in a row at each breakpoint. We go through demonstrations of these practice shots in our video, "How to Practice and Understanding the Move."

Once you feel confident that your move is subconscious, that it's refined and nearly perfect on single quartering and crossing targets within 30 yards (and you're able to back that feeling up by breaking 10 in a row at each breakpoint,) you should begin to add report pairs from station one and five, with the trap still locked down.

At about this point in your learning curve, you'll probably feel confident enough to challenge your friends to a sporting clays round (actually, you likely already have) or even try your hand at a local tournament. If so, that's great. Go and do these things. Have fun but don't get down on yourself, because you're only at the beginning of your journey in this sport.

If you are shooting a tourney, however, try to get into the habit of not thinking about any mechanics during these competitive shoots. Concentrate 100 percent on your plan before you set up to shoot in the stand and 100 percent on the front of the target when you're set up. If you have to score sloppy, score sloppy. Your job is to break targets; you can change mechanics and make your shots prettier during your next practice session.

After you shoot a round for score, you should have some glaring aspects of your game that need work, and they'll likely be on targets within 30 yards. In your practice sessions from here on out, pick one of these weaknesses per session to work on. Go into each practice with a specific goal, for example, "Today, I'm only going to practice left-to-right quartering targets. I'm going to shoot 150 of them and I'm going to work on breaking 60 percent to 70 percent of them late because that gave me the most trouble at the last shoot."

Have a specific goal for each practice session. You can only improve when you have isolated the problem. Find out what you can't do, and practice it. People often practice their strengths, not their weaknesses. The only way you're going to get better is through failure, so go out and make your weaknesses your strengths. You should be trying to create a well-rounded game, meaning the same ability level on all targets. When this occurs, your improvement will accelerate.

Will you eventually need to practice 50-yard crossers? Of course you will, but you'll do yourself a huge favor by first refining your move on close targets, getting confident that anything within 30 yards is yours. We've found that practicing only "hard" targets often gives shooters an excuse to miss. Instead of blaming the quality of their move and mount, they can blame the misses on the difficulty of the target.

One last thing: The right approach to practice depends a lot on attitude. This is something we haven't talked about a lot yet, but the more you progress, the more important it becomes. If you work on maintaining a positive attitude in your practice sessions and integrate that into your routine, you will be surprised at how easy hitting clays becomes. Attitude has more to do with success and failure than any one thing.

"** Just because you are shooting pairs doesn't mean you should abandon your routine or your plan for each stand.**"

CHAPTER   16
Shooting pairs

We're sure you've followed our advice and started with a simple practice routine at a skeet range, a trap field, or on a local clays course before attacking pairs, haven't you? No, you wouldn't dare try to shoot pairs before mastering singles, would you?

Sure … we know the truth. You move too fast, Grasshopper. You've been naughty and we know it.

It's okay, all of us are trigger-happy yahoos deep down — it's part of the fun in this sport. But we admonish you to take us seriously when we say you should make a quality, subconscious move your first priority. Even the master-class shooters are still constantly working on the fundamentals, trying to perfect and maintain an already good move and mount.

When you do get to pairs, or after you've already tackled them and are having trouble, we've come up with a phrase that needs to stay in your head if you want to have success: ***Eyes first, then the gun***.

When shooting pairs it is critical after breaking the first target, your eyes move to the second target ***before*** moving the gun. This is what it should look like.

First target is broken.

Eyes move to find second target.

Eyes focus on the second target.

Gun moves to second target and target is broken.

IF IT AIN'T BROKE, FIX IT!

For all pairs, this is the first thing we tell our students. Most shooters have a strong tendency to push the gun immediately toward the second target after they hit the first. (They do this even though they don't know exactly where the second target is because they haven't seen it!) This does two things: It makes them rush, and it pulls their eyes to the barrel of the gun. The barrel begins to control the eyes instead of the other way around. We cannot stress enough how much risk looking at the barrel introduces into your shot. Every success and every failure in clay sports is rooted in focus on the target. It is crucial to get your eyes on that second bird, and it probably wouldn't hurt to focus on the front edge before you move to it with the gun.

Any gun movement prior to focus on the target is wasted and increases risk by the cube. You're making it three times harder for yourself if you move the gun first. Even if the eyes and gun go for the second target at the same time, the target is harder to lock on to, and the gun will out-swing the bird even though you are looking at it. This can be illustrated at home. Take an unloaded shotgun and mount it on an object. Next, move your eyes and the gun, at the same time, to another object. You can feel how much momentum the gun has; you can't hold it back and you swing past the second object. Try it again, but this time move your eyes to the object first, then the gun. Less muzzle movement, huh? This is because the gun has a specific place to go and it stops on the target. *Eyes first, then the gun*.

1/10 Of A Second

The other mental chant we recommend when shooting pairs is *1/10 of a second*. Your eyes need to be on that second target within 1/10 of a second after breaking the first. Build it into a battle hymn.

Make sure, though, that you move your *eyes* quickly, not your body. You need to rapidly lock on to the leading edge of that second target with your eyes, not your body. Speed in a shot comes from the efficiency of the move, not from how fast you swing the muzzles. This is a common mistake. Most beginning and intermediate shooters move too much and too fast during the move and mount, and shooting pairs makes them move even faster. We can almost guarantee that you usually have more time than you think when you're shooting pairs, and it's always easier to move faster with relaxed muscles. Don't rush … try slowing down and notice how when you slow down … the targets also seem to slow down. Remember … slow … down … see the bird … trust your eyes.

Dismount or Not Dismount?

If, on the second bird, you have time to bring the gun away from your face, our suggestion is to do so. Like we said, the first thing you need to do is see and focus on the bird. If the gun stays against your face as you move to the second target, your eyes will go to the barrel of the gun. Your eyes naturally go to the fastest-moving thing in the picture, and if you move the gun to the target faster than the speed of the target, your eyes will go to the gun. (Sound familiar?) The most important thing, no matter how much time there is between shots, is to make your eyes find and focus on the front of the second bird — before you move the gun to the second bird.

On two outgoing targets, you won't have time to dismount and get to the other bird. You need to find a breakpoint for the first target, pull the trigger no matter what, find the second target with your eyes, move the gun to it, and pull the trigger. You can slightly pull your face from the stock of the gun to find the target, or you can take your eyes immediately to the place where you can see the second target and then move the gun. These

In some instances it is necessary to raise your head off the stock to find the second target of a pair. This is what it should look like.

In some instances the gun must be dismounted to acquire the second target of a pair. Whether the gun is dismounted or not in the transition between the first and second targets of a pair, you must focus on the second target **before** you move the gun to it or you will see the gun and miss the target.

First target is broken.

Head is raised to find the second target.

Second target is acquired and focused on.

Gun moves to second target and target is broken.

movements are illustrated in our video, "Strategy and How to Play the Game."

If you have a quick outgoing target and a real slow incoming target, you should dismount the gun. They are two different moves — fast outgoing and slow incoming. If you don't take the gun away from your face to see the incoming target clearly, the gun will move into your line of sight and your eyes will go to it. Your focus then shifts to the gun and not the target. This does not mean you should completely dismount, bringing the gun down all the way. It just means you should separate your eyes from the gun so you can focus on only the target. You want an efficient move of the gun to the target — any extra movement will increase the risk of missing the target. *See* the target, move to it, and pull the trigger. Always, always, always: *Eyes first, then the gun.*

Don't Forget Breakpoints

Just because you are shooting pairs doesn't mean you should abandon your routine or your plan for each stand. When you ask for your "show pair," you need to decide on two focal points and two breakpoints. That's right, four points: 1) where you will focus on and see the first bird; 2) where you will break the first bird; 3) where your eyes will go to pick up the second bird; and 4) where you will break the second bird.

Treat each target in a pair as if it were a single — meaning, for the second bird you need to find a focal point along its flight path that your eyes can go to after you break the first bird. Pick something specific like a tree branch, and make sure it is not something between you and the bird's flight path; the bird should always be closer to you than your focal point. When you finish with the first target, your eyes will have a specific point to move to immediately, which will make your eyes still, which will allow them to pick up the second target faster, which will give you more time.

If you don't pick a specific focal point, your eyes will be moving around longer, searching for the bird; when your eyes are moving everything in the picture is moving, and you won't pick up the target as well or as quickly.

We find this is a problem for older shooters who complain about not being able to pick up the second target of a pair. As we age and our arms become shorter (isn't that why it feels like we have to hold the newspaper farther and farther away to read it?), whether we want to admit it to ourselves or not, our vision, like the "old grey mare," just ain't what it used to be. As a result, we must become *more* specific with the focal points on the second birds of all pairs. Make sure your eyes are still in the correct focal point for the second bird. Without that commitment, your eyes will be moving and you will *not* see the target as quickly, if at all.

True Pairs

No presentation reveals the importance of a good plan and a consistent routine like a true pair. The key to success lies in your approach. When you're shooting true pairs at a course, you should try to break the first bird of every true pair in the same place at each station. Why? Well, let's say we're shooting a 100-bird course, with 10 stations and five pairs at each station. For every true pair, if you break the first bird in the same spot, is the second bird not the same? But if you break the first bird in a different spot every time, you're forcing yourself to break the second bird in a different spot every time. So you can shoot 10 pairs, five times each, with a consistent breakpoint on each bird, or you can shoot 50 pairs, all different. We don't know about you, but we are going to kill the first bird of each pair in exactly the same place every time. We would much rather shoot 10 pairs five times each instead of 50 different pairs. If you want to consistently break targets, you must be consistent with what you're doing in the stand.

Hint: When taking a show pair on a true pair presentation, instead of looking from one target to the next, focus your eyes between them so you can pick up the line and speed relationship of both targets.

Excessive Follow-Through

Excessive movement creates risk on any shot. Excessive conscious follow-through will kill you on true pairs especially. Follow-through is merely the momentum left in the gun after the target breaks. After all, the reason the gun is moving is because you are focused on the target and the target is moving, right? When the target blows up, why should the gun need to keep moving? You have to pull the trigger, and the shot has to leave the barrel before the target can be broken, correct? There is nothing you can do after the shot cloud leaves the barrel to affect the placement of the shot. It's already gone.

Even with these facts, which come straight from the laws of physics, we constantly see people trying to consciously create follow-through after the trigger is pulled, thinking that it helps with their consistency. Au contraire. Conscious excess follow-through increases risk not only on the first shot of a true pair, but also on the second.

Every ounce of conscious follow-through (employed after the trigger is pulled) must be overcome to make the transition visually and mechanically to the second shot. We find that the reason people employ conscious follow-through is because they become too aware of the gun or the lead. At the last second before they pull the trigger they realize the bird has gotten too close to the gun. At this instant they panic, pull the trigger, and slash the muzzles out away from the target.

This movement is erratic at best and will never be the same from one bird to the next. The birds are the same; the move will be anything but the same.

When the target explodes, there is no reason to keep the gun moving. Once the target is gone, your move for that shot is over, Zorro. It is now time to visually acquire the second target and make a move to break it. You increase your risk when you give any excessive conscious movement to the gun — especially excessive follow-through.

Pair Practice

Here's a great way to practice training your eyes for pairs: Go to a sporting clays course or a five-stand and find a teal target you can hit consistently. You're going to be shooting singles, but put a cylinder choke in your bottom barrel and a full choke in the top. From a distance of about 25 yards, shoot the teal on the way up with the cylinder choke, find the biggest piece of the target after you break it, and shoot it with your second shot. This trains your eyes to go to the second bird before you move the gun. It forces you — you can't move your gun before your eyes because you don't know where the biggest piece will be, so you can't anticipate it.

This is not a natural move. It must be learned, so don't get all pissy if you're not nailing it right off the bat. And remember, it must be the biggest piece, not just any piece.

Teal Part II

Speaking of teal, it's probably a good idea to revisit the topic now that you've had some time to absorb the first part. The springing teal is difficult for most shooters to break consistently, so we think it's a good idea to continue the discussion here.

Another mistake we often see people make on this trajectory is picking a hold point that is too low when taking the target near its peak. If your focal point is close to the trap and your hold point is just above that, the gun will be in catch-up mode when the target appears. The eyes have already given the brain the wrong data because they've read the target as a 50 mph bird requiring a lot of lead. But by the time you pull the trigger, the bird has become a much slower quartering target, requiring very little lead. This means you'll be chasing after the target with the muzzles, and we all know what happens when you chase the target.

A higher hold point will yield more consistent results because it allows you to move the gun more slowly, which allows you to be more precise. By choosing a hold point halfway or more up the flight path of the target, and focusing the eyes just below the hold point, you will visually slow the target and your move will not be rushed. Approached this way, the teal has become a much slower, non-transitional target that can be broken with less gun movement and more consistency.

Also, remember the importance of keeping the muzzles out of the target's flight line. If you're right-handed, hold the muzzles slightly off to the right of the flight line, if you're a lefty, hold it to the left.

Now, we don't want you to think that shooting the teal near its peak is the only method you're ever going to need. Sporting clays target setters are shooters, too, you see, and they want to pull you out of your comfort zone. When they set up target pairs involving teal, they sometimes make it so the easiest way to break both targets is to shoot the teal going up or coming down. It is necessary to learn all three ways, going up, coming down, and near the peak.

Going Up

Taking a teal on the way up requires some forward allowance. Hold your gun almost at the breakpoint and move your eyes down closer to the trap. When you see the bird, merge the muzzles over the top of the target, trust that the gun is in the right place, and pull the trigger. It's a fast quartering move and there will be some vertical push to the muzzles, but not a lot.

Both hands, when moving to shoot a teal on the way up, must go up. The lateral move is up when shooting a teal. If you're a right-handed person who has a lot of right hand in your move, the gun butt will come up faster than the muzzles, and this will bring the muzzles down. You'll miss the shot low. Eyes low and gun high. Meet the teal at the breakpoint.

At the Peak

Trying to shoot the teal at its "peak" increases risk. This is because the peak is a relative term. The only way you know the target is at its peak is after it has started to fall. So either shoot it just before the peak or just after the peak.

Like we said before, when the teal is at its peak you don't want to have any extra gun speed because this target is slowing down dramatically. Hold the gun up high, almost at the breakpoint. Your eyes will need to focus between the barrel and the trap. When you see the target, move to it. The biggest problem most people have is that their gun is moving faster than the bird and they fly right over the top of this target. Make the move softer and more vertical if you are breaking it just before the peak, and make a soft insertion to the lead if breaking it just after the peak.

Coming Down

Of all the ways to shoot a teal, many shooters will try to avoid shooting the dropping teal. Droppers can be problematic, but only if you make them that way. To consistently break dropping teal, your focus must be on the bottom of the target, and you should begin your move much later in the flight path when the target begins to fall. If you are looking at the middle or at the whole target, you will not hit this dropper. Don't move your muzzles up with the bird and then back down, trying to mirror the arch. You can watch the bird as it goes up, but don't move on it until it begins to fall. If you are taking the bird just after the peak, your quartering move will involve less movement than if you choose to take it as it nears the ground, because the target speed increases from the peak to the ground.

Here again, gun speed and target speed need to be the same. You can either move the gun to the bottom of the target and then pull away from it, you can insert the gun under the target and stabilize the picture (match the gun speed with target speed) as the target falls, or you can simply insert the gun where you want to break the target, merging with the target at your chosen breakpoint.

While any of these ways will work, the problem with the pull-away, or maintained lead, method is that you don't always have time to go to the bird and play with it. The easier way to hit this target is to move to it, matching target speed and gun speed, put the gun into the lead window (don't check the barrel), and pull the trigger. This move requires a lot of practice to master, but once mastered, it is lethal on all types of droppers.

Understand that what we're telling you here is not a substitute for direct experience. We're sorry that we can't teach you to master this move in a book or a video, but this is one shot you must be able to feel. In fact, this is what learning anything is all about. It's about feel, focus, rhythm, timing, and trust — things that are hard to completely absorb from a book. You can grasp them intellectually and understand the role they play in shooting, but you just aren't going to master them after reading a book. The only way you'll master feel, focus, rhythm, timing, and trust is by learning from an experienced coach who understands them.

In the chapters on practice, we told you to shoot a target at one breakpoint until you are comfortable with it, then master the same target at two other breakpoints. Nothing changes here. Shoot the teal going up until you can do it 10 times in a row, then master taking it on both sides of the peak.

A lot of shooters will practice all three ways but never get comfortable with one; therefore, they never achieve total confidence in hitting the teal all three ways. Don't get on that bull until you've broken the pony.

"Just focus on the center circle and shoot at it. Don't make it so complicated."

CHAPTER 17
That @!#! wabbit*

Elmer Fudd never cursed, but he would have if he'd ever met a sporting clays rabbit. We've seen it many times. A student comes to us with the fire of frustration in his eyes — a glimmer of insanity. We can tell it's difficult for him to hold in. There's obviously a problem, so we ask him what it is.

That's when he lets fly. "It's that @!#*! rabbit," he says. "I keep shooting in front of that @!#*! rabbit!"

How uncouth.

When a shooter says he's missing the rabbit in front, we know that one of two things is the problem: Either he's not holding focus on the target, or more often, he's moving the gun way too fast. Both are the result of never having good focus prior to beginning the move.

Rabbit targets appear to move faster than they really are because they bounce erratically, and you're never going to see them fly in a straight line like a normal clay. Also, a shooter can

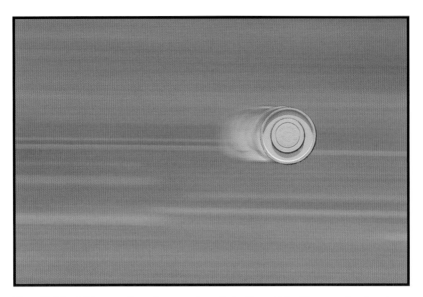

The rabbit target is one of varying speeds and lines. Its front edge is in constant transition. If you can focus on the center circle, the rabbit will appear to slow down and move in a much straighter line.

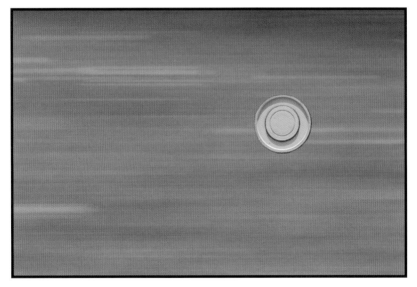

It is the only target where we recommend you look at the center, because the front edge is always changing. The center is always the center. Focus on the center circle before moving your gun, and the rabbit will be much easier to break consistently.

reference the ground, which is not available when the target is in the air. It's like coming in for landing in an airplane; it seems like it's moving faster than it was in the air, even though it's much slower.

Because the rabbit appears faster than it really is, excessive gun speed typically creates misses in front. Even though everything looks right when you pull the trigger, you still miss in front because the gun is going so much faster than the rabbit.

We see this problem most frequently in women (although it happens in some men), and we think it's because most women see lead in terms of inches at the barrel, not feet at the target like most men. More on that later.

Where To Focus

The rabbit target bounces erratically, putting the front edge in constant transition. The easiest way to slow down both the rabbit and the gun is to focus on the center circle of the rabbit and keep yourself from moving until you're locked on to it. The rabbit has a raised center where the manufacturer's logo is stamped. When sharp focus on this circle is achieved, the target will seem to slow down because you are less aware of the background. The target will also seem to straighten out its flight path.

Here's another big thing about rabbits — they come out fast but slow down every time they bounce. Also, the longer they are on the ground (rolling and not hopping), the quicker they slow down. The swing should slow down with the rabbit so the lead picture will be constant and correct. Your move should always mirror the target. Huh, does that sound familiar?

So just focus on the center circle and shoot at it. Don't make it so complicated. Little if any forward allowance is necessary as long as the rabbit target is within 25 to 30 yards. Rabbits at a greater distance require lead. You will miss in front if your swing speed is not as slow as the movement of the rabbit. Any target at a distance requires a soft, slow move. Remember: ***Mirror the target speed!***

"How do you know where to put the gun if you are not looking at the target?"

CHAPTER   18
When you miss

It will happen, Sweet Cheeks, and how you deal with it plays a big part in how often. Rule number one: Don't worry about *where* you missed the target, except regarding how it reflects on your move or on your focus. Too many people concern themselves with where they missed the target. Go to any clays course and we guarantee you'll hear something like this: "Hell, Homer, you were seven feet over that one," or "You need to lead it by about three more feet, Cletus."

Where Cletus missed is irrelevant, and telling him to lead it by three more feet will only get him deeper into mechanical thinking. Instead, he should be concerned with *why* he missed, and what to change in order to hit the next target.

A shooter's focus must be 100 percent on seeing and hitting the target. When you miss, you should strive to understand why, not where.

As to the question of *why*, remember when we told you about the three reasons for a miss? (Chapter 2) It always comes back to these things: Lack of focus, gun speed didn't match the target speed, or a flaw in the gun mount. And, once you have worked on perfecting your move and mount for a couple of months, you're down to two big reasons.

The next time you miss, ask yourself, "What did I see — target, gun or lead?" If the answer isn't "target," then lack of focus is the reason you missed. If you're sure you saw only the target, ask yourself, "Did the gun feel like it was moving and mounting the same direction and speed as the target?" When this occurs, everything should feel like it is moving in slow motion. If your answer is "no," gun speed is the culprit.

We realize this sounds way too simple, but in our experience it is fact. More targets are missed due to lack of target focus and improper gun speed than all other reasons combined (that includes eye dominance), especially when we're dealing with shooters who have a decent mount. If the correct lead is not applied at the correct place and your gun speed is not the same as the target's speed, then the right lead becomes the wrong lead.

In analyzing a miss, those people who begin to blame the sudden onset of cross-dominance are in the right zip code with their analysis; they understand the problem is with the eyes, but they're making it more complicated than it needs to be. If they're shooters with a good move who average upwards of 70, we can discount eye dominance or a faulty move as the culprit. They're shooting too well for true cross-dominance to be the problem. Right there we know it's either improper focus or gun speed. So, when someone like this comes to us and says they think they're having eye dominance problems because they're missing easy, close targets, the first thing we ask them to do is shoot a 25-yard crosser.

When they miss we'll ask them, "What did you see?"

"I'm shooting targets great and all of a sudden I see the gun," is usually how the answer goes. Our question then is, "How do you know where to put the gun if you are not looking at the target?"

The deer-in-the-headlights look follows. They realize that the last thing they saw before they pulled the trigger was the gun. The dawn breaks.

The reason they're missing the easy close targets is not intermittent eye dominance, it's that they're spending too much time trying to locate the barrel to put it in front of the target. Not necessary. Just put it somewhere in front. The shotgun is a very forgiving instrument because of the width of the pattern. If you are looking at the front of the target, the gun will get there. Don't try for an exact lead or that conscious-thought thing enters into the shot. That will put you behind. Be more concerned about your focus on the target and let the mind-body computer do its job. Tempo, baby! Tempo!

Maintaining Focus Through The Shot

Target focus is a simple thing. It's either there or it isn't. You either never had it or you had it but lost it. When you've analyzed a miss and discovered focus is the problem, think about what you felt before the shot. If you realize you never had focus, the solution is simple — get it before you move the gun. This is accomplished through pre-shot routine, by holding your eyes still on the focal point as you call "pull."

If your eyes were still before you called "pull" but you lost focus during the shot, the basic move of the gun was probably wrong. In 99 percent of instances, the move was too fast and it pulled your primary focus off the target and onto the gun or the lead. This should lead you to re-examine your move and might suggest that you need to go back to the basics, or at least move your hold point out.

Remember, your eyes instinctively go to the fastest-moving object in the scene. When you have focus and lose it, the gun has moved faster than the target and has pulled your focus off the target and on to the gun. But it sure is a pretty gun, isn't it?

John Higgins, an Englishman, one-time chief instructor for the National Sporting Clays Association and a damn fine gent, said something that is becoming clearer to us as we teach 1,500 to 2,000 people each year in our clinics, seminars, and hourly lessons. He said, "You Americans are too intent on breaking the target, therefore you never learn the basic move well enough to achieve consistency of any sort." Roger Silcox, another great British shooting instructor, has echoed this sentiment for a long time.

Those old boys have gotten smarter over the years.

MasterCard Journey Of Improvement

The MasterCard route is one that a lot of people take when they begin to develop a consistent move and mount but still can't seem to score above the 60 to 70 range. When they analyze their misses, they rarely go with the simple explanation — that they didn't have target focus — and they begin to blame their equipment. It is during this stage that a visit to what we call the Black Hole typically takes place. What is the Black Hole? It is the place that all the monkey-see monkey-dos, who have degrees in self-diagnostic science, gather to improve their games.

They try things like changing gun fit by installing a moveable butt plate and cheek piece (which they promptly get so far out of adjustment it's absolutely impossible to mount or shoot without injury, much less hit anything). They install a florescent bead sight to make the gun more visible when they're shooting. They try faster shells in an attempt to see less lead. They try different chokes to manipulate the size of the shot cloud, when they didn't put the gun where it needed to be in the first place.

We read an article a while back that covered the advances that have been made in golf equipment in recent years, exotic materials, oversized club heads, shafts with different amounts of flex, etc. The writer went to great lengths to describe the advantages of all the combinations. However, at the end of the article he wrote something very profound: "If your swing is bad you will hit bad shots. Nothing will improve your game as much as improving your swing."

This is so true in shotgunning as well. We see people buying all sorts of products to make them better shots, but the sad thing is, if they would spend more time working on the basic swing dynamics and mechanics, their game would improve dramatically. But this is not as easy as using the old charge card to buy gadgets.

Typically, after a thousand dollars or so, the people in the Black Hole finally stop listening to themselves or to their friends and get to an experienced teacher or coach.

Don't worry. If you come to us, we're not going to take all your toys away. We're not against having good equipment. Gil's uncle, Dusty Garrett, told him once that 90 percent of the fun in anything is having the best equipment you could possibly afford. Having the correct lens color for your shooting environment is important. Using the correct chokes and load is important. Having a gun that you are proud of, and that fits you, is of equal importance. We find that people shoot guns that they are proud of better than guns they aren't.

> **Free advice will always cost you more than what you paid for it.**

However, we're sure we could give Bobby Fowler a gun he'd never seen or shot before, with an unknown choke in it, with ammunition he's not accustomed to shooting, and he could still break a 30-yard crosser 10 times in a row. Why? He has a smooth, subconscious swing, the key words being *smooth* and *subconscious*.

It's the consistency of the move that breaks the targets. You don't have to be smooth to be a great shot, but all great shots are smooth.

The more precise and consistent your swing and mount are, the easier it is to move the gun with the speed and direction of the target. The more the gun mirrors the target line and speed, the easier it is to maintain critical laser focus on the target. The better the focus on the target, the more targets you will break. When you miss targets you think you should hit, it's usually time to go back to fundamentals.

Emote The Solution and Have a Short Memory

Quite a few people overlook the importance of the mental side of this game. It's especially critical when you miss and when you're trying to fix something. It's good to analyze why you missed a target, but before you shoot the next one, you shouldn't be thinking about what you did wrong. Think instead about what you will change to hit the next target. This will be a positive thought, not a negative one.

Do not emote the problem after a miss. Emote the solution. Don't say, "Damn it! I made a shitty mount." Say, "Okay, I'm going to have a perfect mount."

A good round of clays is the sum of all the shots, both good and bad. The bad shots are just as much a part of the game as the good ones. If dwelt on, they will perpetuate themselves, if learned from and forgotten, they eliminate themselves. Emotions are the gatekeepers to the learning process and the performance process.

So remember only the good shots … if you remember the bad ones, you will see them over and over again.

> *"There is not one perfect method to use with a shotgun because of the difference in individual strengths and weaknesses."*

CHAPTER   19
Other Methods

Okay, now we're ready to talk about other methods of shooting, and the things that increase or decrease risk in each of them.

A nice thing about the technique we teach is it doesn't matter if you are shooting clays or live birds — it works for everything. This is because we've found that the root of almost every problem in shotgunning is conscious awareness of the gun. The basis of our technique is focus on the leading edge of the bird, and it deemphasizes anything that causes the eyes to go to the gun, like checking the lead or moving the gun faster than the target speed. We spend more time getting our students to focus on the front of the clay or the head of the bird than worrying about how to get there. If you are worried about a specific lead on a target, you will have to look at the barrel to check the distance. Once that happens, you take your focus off the target, place it on the gun, and you stop — and the bird is gone.

As to the method, it really doesn't matter which one you use as long as you get the gun moving the same speed as the bird and pull the trigger in front. Our technique is compatible with any method that allows you to do this, and we'll teach you any method you want to learn. The video we mentioned earlier in our shameless plug ("How To Practice and Understanding the Move") has a great section that shows how the various methods look from the bird's-eye view. It was tough strapping the camera on that pigeon, but it was worth it.

There will be times with any method when the bird will surprise you by getting in front of your gun. Instead of frantically putting the gun to your cheek and trying to find the bird, mount the gun at the proper point in front of the bird, and pull the trigger.

Most important of all, pull the trigger when the stock gets to your face. This will allow you to keep focus on the target, not the gun. Your eyes will go to the fastest moving thing in the picture. They have no choice. So keep the gun out of the picture until you are ready to pull the trigger. If you are too concerned with the method you're using to get there, your focus will shift and your conscious mind will guide the shot. We all know what happens when the conscious, doubting mind gets involved — you miss. The conscious mind works 3/10th of a second behind real time. The subconscious mind works instantly. Which one do you want working for you?

There is not one perfect method to use with a shotgun because of the difference in individual strengths and weaknesses. That said, there are things that increase or decrease risk in any method. Here are a few descriptions of the typical "methods" we see people using, their risks and benefits.

Swing-through

Swing-through is a viable, but unforgiving method. It carries with it the greatest amount of risk. By definition, it is a move that involves the muzzles swinging through the target from behind. Instead of merging with the target in front, it is a deliberate swing from behind.

When mastered, swing-through can be especially effective in hunting situations because live birds will accelerate as you mount, while sporting clays targets will slow down. It can be dangerous here too, however, because many hunters tend to see the flash of the bird and throw the gun up quickly, instead of easing through the bird.

In sporting clays, swing-through is effective on some second shots. If, when you kill the first target, your gun is behind the second target and there's no time for a dismount, a swing-through move can often be to your advantage.

When we teach swing-through, we still admonish our students to employ the basic technique of merging with the target. We find that the closer the tempo of the move is to the tempo of the target, the less visual confusion occurs. For example, in our car analogy, think of it as merging just behind a car and putting on just enough gas to slowly pass it. If you move your muzzles through the target at one mph faster than the target, you'll have more success than you will moving them 10 mph faster than the target because your eyes will not be so attracted to the muzzles if they're only moving slightly faster than the target. And don't neglect your breakpoint, focal point, and routine with this method. It doesn't matter what method you use, if you look at the gun and try to measure the lead, you're finished.

Swing-through shooters are either heroes or zeroes. They're either really good or really bad, and let us say we've seen "really bad" much more than "really good." This is because the success of this method depends wholly on timing. The gun spends precious little time in the lead, so it demands perfection. Swing-through shooters typically have trouble with long crossers, curling birds, window shots, and second birds on a true pair. They'll top out at 75 to 78 and have a score differential of 11 to 18 birds.

Remember, to have any success with this method, muzzle speed must be very close to bird speed. This makes it easier to focus on the target, and the timing is more forgiving. Still, we don't recommend it as a primary mode of attack for sporting clays targets.

> **Score differential is the difference between a shooter's high scores and low scores.**

Mount and Chase

The mount and chase can sometimes be a variation of the swing-through method, but it's not a good variation if hitting the target is important to you. The mount-and-chaser does not merge muzzles with target, from in front or behind. Instead, he mounts the gun and then tries to catch up from behind.

Even if the move is really good, if the mount comes up vertically (assume we're talking about a crossing bird) it will be way behind the target from the get-go. You can't mirror the bird at this point because it's already past you. The gun has to be in front of the target to break it, so why would you want to put it behind? This makes for an ugly picture. If you don't want to check it out on our video, make a video of yourself shooting this way, or have a friend watch you.

The move will always be much faster than the target speed, and this makes your eyes go to the gun. Then as your eyes move between the target and the barrel, the move begins to resemble the second hand on a quartz watch: tick … tick … tick. Bird to barrel … bird to barrel … bird to barrel.

When you watch yourself or someone else make this move, you'll see that when you're behind the target, it controls you. Only when you're in front do you have control.

Rushing Vertical

This is a cousin to the mount and chase, but in this case, the vertical move is not only made first, it's also made extremely fast. So when the muzzles come up, they come up too far, causing the butt of the gun to drop, and now everything is in chaos. The shooter has to bring the muzzles back down, bring the butt back up, and catch up to the crossing bird. The eyes go to the gun rather than staying on the bird, and the mount has already caused visual confusion.

The fast vertical mount on this move is usually a result of the shooter rushing because he knows he's already behind the bird, or he wants to get the gun mounted in a hurry so he can chase and check the lead.

Usually the rush to catch up makes the shooter lean either to the left or right and throws the body out of balance. This is bad because, like we talked about in the stance section, the body's strongest instinct is balance. By throwing yourself out of balance, you force the subconscious to concentrate on getting you back in balance, making target focus impossible.

Pull-away

In the pull-away or pull-ahead method, the shooter mounts the gun on the target, but pulls ahead of the target before pulling the trigger. Instead of mounting behind the target, like a swing-through shooter, the pull-away shooter mounts on the target and uses the pull-away to get the shot in front of the bird. As with swing-through, it's risky because it involves the muzzles moving faster than the target.

The pull-away can be pretty effective on longer targets, and some people like it on medium targets, but it's not very effective on several other presentations, such as curling birds, window shots, and quick true pairs. Good pull-away shooters tend to average 78 to 84 and have a score differential of eight to 12 birds. As with swing-through shooters, the gun of a pull-away shooter spends only the last five percent of the shot far enough ahead of the bird to break it.

Our best advice for success with this method is to mount the gun slightly under the bird or just in front, and match the target speed for a fraction of a second before pulling ahead. If the gun is mounted just under or just ahead of the bird and stays with the bird for a moment before the gun pulls ahead of the target, we find that the eyes tend to stay with the bird. If the gun comes up too fast or mounts directly on the bird, we find the eyes tend to move away with the gun on the pull-away.

Last Second Pull-away

This variation on the pull-away is almost too horrible to include. The name we gave it is pretty much the only description you need, but to fill in the details, this "method" involves a shooter pushing the gun way ahead of the bird at the end of the shot. We're talking tons of conscious follow-through. Even if the original move is pretty good, when the gun comes up on the line of a crossing target, the shooter starts checking the lead. Then in a panic, last-second move, he jerks the gun out in front of the bird. You can't expect consistency with this move.

Slashing Move

Another doozy. The slasher can be someone who uses either swing-through or pull-away methods. This guy would be good in a swordfight, but the problem is he's got a shotgun in his hands. We see this all the time, and it's a wild sight. The shooter starts behind the bird, and his eyes are going from the gun to the target the whole time. The swing is typically very fast, somewhere between Mach one and warp four, and there is absolutely no hope of focus on the target because the muzzles are moving so fast. Save this one for fencing.

"The game of sporting clays 'ain't no thinking thing.' It goes a little deeper than that."

CHAPTER 20

Introduction to the Voice

Actually, the voice needs no introduction. You have known the voice as long as you have understood words. You need the voice to remind you it's time to do your taxes, to memorize anything, or to keep you from driving 90 even when it's a straight road and there's nobody around. You need the voice to translate the words in this book into a solid grasp of the fundamental mechanics of shotgunning.

Once you achieve excellence in mechanics, however, the voice is no longer your friend.

The voice of conscious doubt is how we usually refer to it, although it doesn't always obviously manifest itself as doubt. It is essentially the conscious mind. It is the constant babble of thoughts that run through your head, the ongoing mental conversation you have with yourself whenever your mind isn't focused. Why isn't the voice helpful to shotgunners? Well, try for one second to stop it. Try to refrain from thinking about anything, just for a few seconds.

Not easy, is it? Welcome to the next level of shotgunning.

No Thinking Thing

Now, we don't know if Trace Adkins is aware of it, but he wrote a country song about shotgunning. In it he says, "This ain't no thinking thing." The boy's got sense. The game of sporting clays "ain't no thinking thing." It goes a little deeper than that.

Does this sound familiar? You've started to run a stand, or you've been shooting very well during a competition, then you think to yourself, "Wow, if I continue to shoot this way, I could score in the 80s." Then you end up shooting like crap. You have just been victimized by the voice.

Ideally, after you step in the stand and say, "I'm going to see it there, and break it there," you should have no more thoughts running through your mind, especially thoughts about mechanics. The problem is, you'll get so caught up in trying not to think, you'll end up thinking. You'll be thinking about not thinking. This is heavy stuff. Some people spend their whole lives trying to conquer conscious thought. There's probably some Tibetan monk sitting on a mountain struggling with it right now.

We don't expect you to become a Zen master or a holy yogi, although it probably wouldn't hurt. As an alternative to blocking out the voice, we suggest you tie it up.

"And how, O Enlightened Ones, do you suggest we do that?" you ask. (Are we sensing sarcasm?)

You tie up the voice with two things: Focus and routine. You tie it up by letting your subconscious mind take over, by "shooting instinctively." We could probably write an entire series of books on shooting instinctively and all that it entails, but we just don't have the space to go into full detail here. Not to worry, we will concentrate heavily on this subject in book two of the series.

For now, we'll concentrate on pre-shot routine. It will probably take you some time to develop a consistent pre-shot routine, because it will take you some time to figure out what makes you comfortable and allows you to focus best. Your pre-shot routine will be unique, but all good routines have some common elements.

- *First, it should obviously be consistent.* Once you figure out what works, do it the same way every time. If it makes you feel comfortable to take two gulps of water before you step into a stand, take two gulps of water every time (although you may be making a few more trips to the toilet.) If you want to integrate deep breathing, do that.
- *It should be positive.* Don't neglect your attitude when coming up with a pre-shot routine. Saying to yourself, "I'm never going to hit this target," just before you call "pull" will be effective if missing the targets is your goal. It sounds simple, but you would be surprised how many people give themselves negative thoughts before they call "pull." The last thing you think will be the first thing that happens. We recommend giving yourself something positive to think just before you call pull, for example, "front edge," or "laser focus."
- *It shouldn't end when you pull the trigger.* In practice, be mindful of how long it takes you to reload between shots, how long it takes you to call "pull" for the next bird. You want this time to be consistent. You don't want it to take four seconds to load and call "pull" the first time and 12 seconds the next. Making this steady will help you develop a rhythm in your routine. This way, you'll begin to do it automatically.
- *It should be re-started if interrupted.* Don't be afraid to begin your routine again if something breaks your focus. If someone comes

up to talk or something takes your mind off hitting the target, stop — start the routine again. Open your gun, take the shells out, and step back in the stand if you need to. You will find that it takes very little for your mind to wander, and, unfortunately, it doesn't take much for the conscious mind to get involved. The conscious mind doubts what you are doing. You must keep the voice quiet and occupied. Do this by staying in your routine, confident that your plan will work.

• *It should be practiced.* Routine is something you must practice … it doesn't just come. Practice staying in your routine and shooting 10 targets in a row. This way, if you go to a tournament that only has six to shoot per stand, you are ahead of the game.

Watching professional basketball players shoot free throws is a good way to see routine in action. The good ones do the same thing every time, down to how many times they dribble, the stance they use, and what they do just before the shot. If you watch their lips you will see some saying things to themselves (we'd bet it's positive) and one NBA player even blows the basket a kiss before the shot. This is pretty smart when you think about it; this is a positive action, and maybe it reminds him that he's just playing a game!

If you find yourself getting too tense or serious before a shot, it isn't a bad idea to develop something playful into your routine. Tailor it to your own strengths, and your routine will pay big dividends.

«The more your visual process includes things other than mechanics, the more effective it will become.»

CHAPTER   21
Introduction to visualization

If there is anything close to magic in this game we play, if there is anything in this book that will work miracles not only in your shotgunning, but in your life, it's visualization. We're not peddling snake oil here, either. If you put honest and regular effort into visualization, you will find out for yourself what a dramatic shortcut it can be to peak performance and how much faster and more effectively it will help you develop your skills.

We were tempted to make this section Chapter One because we believe in it so strongly, but we decided that mastering the basic move and mount, and some field experience, are essential before visualization can really be used to full advantage. You have to know what it feels, sounds, smells, and looks like to break a target before you can properly visualize it. Once you have been to a range and broken a target, however, we recommend using visualization on a daily basis.

"That's great," you might say, "but what exactly is visualization?"

Visualization is basically advanced daydreaming. It is using your ability to form mental pictures in a focused manner, and orchestrating these mental images in a way that will assist you in achieving a goal. In its base form, it's every sexual fantasy your tilted little mind has ever conjured up. In sports performance, it's about taking that inherent ability to fantasize and using it in a way to elevate your game to levels you didn't know existed.

A lot of our colleagues thought we were spewing some crazy hocus-pocus when we first began teaching what we had learned about vision and visualization. The concept of focusing on the front of the target and trusting the subconscious computer was hard for some to accept. When we talked about instinctive shooting some "experts" assumed that what we meant was no thought, no plan, no method, or approach. Boy, were they products of their own mechanical thinking!

Mechanical thinking will get you only so far. Thinking mechanically about lead in exact terms, or even trying to visualize exact leads by looking at 2X4's cut to specific lengths at given distances only causes conscious awareness of the gun and swing mechanics. When you visualize conscious mechanics, that's what you get. When you visualize targets blowing up in the breakpoint, however, that is what you get. The more your visual process includes things other than mechanics, the more effective it will become.

As with instinctive shooting, the amount we have to say about visualization cannot fit in a 10-page chapter. It is a subject that gets a lot of our energy. We have written articles about it for *Sporting Clays* magazine, and many of our call-in Coaching Hour sessions have been devoted entirely to visualization. The articles and Coaching Hour CDs are archived and updated on our website (www.ospschool.com), and we urge you to check them out. It is a subject we are continually learning more about, and we are planning to devote a large portion of our second book to visualization and the many ways we've found it to be useful.

For now, here is our latest advice on how to get started with a basic visualization routine:

Find a place where you can be alone and without interruptions for 15 to 20 minutes. It's probably better that you go to a fairly dark room so you don't need to squint and aren't tempted to open your eyes. Bring your gun (unloaded!) and find a place in the room where you can swing it around without knocking the pictures off the walls. Close your eyes and picture yourself going through your routine, preparing for a target that is easy for you to hit, one that you've hit many times before.

The more detail you can insert into the scene, the better. If you can imagine the way the wind feels on your face, how warm or cold it is, what it smells like, all these things will enhance your visualization. Now picture yourself stepping into the stand. The view can either be internal (what you would see from your point of view) or external (what someone watching you would see). Imagine the target being launched from the trap … making your move … pulling the trigger. Picture a puff of powder as the target explodes into thousands of pieces.

Concentrate on how it feels to swing the gun. Try to get an enhanced feeling for those swings that are smooth and steady. In your visualization, imagine getting connected through feel to the targets you see yourself breaking. You are mirroring the targets; you are in a perfect rhythm. Continue doing this for 15 or 20 minutes, and try to strip away any negative elements of your move. Try to do it at least once every day. It's okay to think about how your mechanics feel during visualization, but don't think about the actual swing mechanics. Think about how they feel as you visualize. And if 20 minutes is too long, break it up into shorter sessions of five minutes several times a day. Try visualization with and without the gun, and try moving on to different presentations once you gain confidence.

Visualization is like underwear, man, go with whatever feels right. Don't force it. It's going to feel a bit strange at first, so just mess around with it — play with how it feels.

There are really no limits to what you can do with this, but to start, we recommend a simple visualization routine with the goals of perfecting your move and getting connected through feel to the targets. We'll talk more about using visualization (at the range, in other settings, and for other purposes) in the next installment, but for now, chew on it for those 20 minutes a day in your home or at the office. If you experiment with what works best for you, eventually you'll begin to develop your own style of visualization. It's something very personal, like a pre-shot routine, and everyone will have a little different method of visualizing.

Visualize This

Tom Kirchmer came to us in 2002. He was about as coordinated with a shotgun as a cow with a wooden leg. Don't get us wrong, he's a deadly archer and he played college football, but he had no concept of what to do with a shotgun. But Tom was one of the few people who took what we taught him, practiced that and nothing more.

To start, he shot singles, as we advised him. After about three months, we taught him how to shoot pairs. Tom then decided to try visualization. "I had heard about it on the Coaching Hour CDs, but I was a little leery of doing it at my stage," Tom said. "After the first week, Gil told me about using my arms as if I were holding the gun. All of a sudden, in the next two weeks things accelerated rapidly. I have a feeling that visualization helped a whole lot."

We guess so, because when Tom signed up for his first NSCA tournament just a few weeks after that, he shot an 82 and won his class. To put this in perspective, the high score for the day, in all classes, was an 88.

"I felt pretty good about the way it worked," Tom said.

So did we, Tom, so did we.

Some people have trouble with visualization because they're skeptical of it or feel like it's too goofy. They act like we're telling them to rub powdered tiger pizzle into their shooting hands. This ain't black magic folks; we're not asking you to tap into the power of the supernatural. Those people who use it don't go crazy.

Visualization doesn't guarantee perfection, but we have found that the positive results for countless students speak for themselves.

And when the aliens land … they'll agree with us.

"If you're afraid that we will screw you up when you come to a lesson, all we can say is, 'Well, duh!'"

CHAPTER 22
Lessons

We obviously have no problem plugging our own products, the videos, the Coaching Hour CDs and now the book; we're proud of what we have to offer and we stand behind our work, but it is not a plug when we say there is no substitute for hands-on teaching. Yes, this book will bring you along faster in your learning curve if you put effort into its application, and it is one of the most accessible teaching tools — something you can take with you everywhere — but a lesson with an experienced instructor offers an outside perspective on your game, that you can't get with books or videos. This is a fact, and we're not making a pitch when we recommend lessons for shooters of all levels. It won't break our hearts if you take a lesson with another instructor: We can all book only a certain number of lessons each year and still be effective, but we really urge you to make sure the instructor you choose has substantial experience in coaching, deals with *why* you missed, not *where*, and can effectively communicate the things you need to change to shoot better. An experienced coach *teaches* more than he or she shoots.

When To Take The Plunge

One of the most common questions we get regarding lessons is, "When do I know it's time to take one?"

Well, in life, if it ain't broke you don't have to fix it, but in sporting clays, most of the time you can't fix it until you break it. What we mean by this is, if your definition of success in this sport is breaking 50 percent of the targets and you have achieved that level and don't desire to get any better, then don't change a thing. But if you want to improve, you're going to have to break some things, and maybe that means a bad habit that you've developed in your swing mechanics, or changing a certain way of talking to yourself before you call "pull."

Our best advice is to take a lesson when your scores plateau, when you've reached a flat line in your shooting improvement. A few symptoms of a plateau include: having trouble with a particular presentation (you just can't get a handle on it); you can't figure out why you are missing; or you are having chronic trouble with a certain aspect of your game. If the targets aren't breaking, you gotta fix it!

What To Expect

You will have to put effort into the lesson if you expect improvement. Even the most experienced instructors are not miracle workers, and the more committed you are to putting what you learn to practice, the more you will improve. Understand, however, that a shooting problem is not going to get fixed during a lesson. The fundamental concept behind the problem will be understood through shooting and coaching. Then, it is up to you to practice the new concept enough so that it can be incorporated into your game. Once it is subconscious enough to be done without thinking about it, then and only then is it fixed.

How long will the fixing take? A week, two weeks, a month … 300 shots, 500 shots, 1,000? This is determined by your attitude and commitment to push through the misses while you're consciously learning the new concept. Wasn't it Winston Churchill who defined success as going from one failure to another with no loss of enthusiasm?

The most common mistake we see in this phase of learning is that the shooter wants the problem to go away instantly. "Are we there yet?" Only patience, perseverance, and hard work will make the problem go away. Remember, a bad habit, regardless of how good it feels, is still a bad habit. You never break an old habit; you must replace it with a new one. This is the basic difference between advice from other shooters and advice from an experienced coach. A shooter will typically tell you how he or she does it. When you take a shooter's advice, you are limited to how well you can do what they do. A good coach will give you information that will allow you to push your potential upward with the tools you've got and won't expect you to adopt a whole new set of tools.

An experienced instructor also understands that a student's problem rarely stems from incorrect lead. Lead, however, is the first place everyone goes — kind of like a shade tree mechanic who changes the spark plugs on a car that needs a transmission overhaul. Let us repeat: In our instruction, we find that one of three things is most often the root of the problem. In order of frequency and importance, they are:

1. *Lack of focus* on the front of the target
2. *Lack of tempo* — not moving the gun with the speed of the target

3. ***Poor gun mount*** — not mounting the gun correctly to the face

It is more important to know why you missed than where. We even tell our students it is irrelevant where you miss. The only way you get more consistent is to understand ***why***.

We Will Screw You Up

If you're afraid that we will screw you up when you come to a lesson, all we can say is, "Well, duh!"

Isn't that the point? As we've been saying from the get-go, in order to fix something, sometimes you have to break it first.

If you have a bad habit, the only way we can help you to replace it with a good habit is by screwing up the bad habit. Like we said, the last thing anyone should expect is to leave a shooting lesson shooting better! It sounds crazy but it's true: You should expect change when you come to a lesson. Even if it isn't completely broken — fix it!

We find that people who are afraid to change ***believe*** that if they just keep doing the same thing they will get better. Sounds like the definition of insanity to us. If you are doing something the least effective way, it's not going to get more effective just because you do copious amounts of it. You should leave a lesson with an understanding of what's wrong and how to fix it. Then it's up to you to practice what you have learned enough to build confidence and trust in your new move so it can become part of your game. That's when you get better.

How To Prepare

First, admit to yourself that when you ain't breaking them, it's broke. Then, the best thing to do to enhance the effectiveness of your lesson is to practice your move and mount beforehand. Go back to Chapter 10 and go through the exercises. In that chapter, we said it's easier to instruct a person who has a few kinks in his move than one who has no move at all. We weren't kidding, and although we don't mind starting from scratch, we feel that your money will be better spent if you go through the basics of a move and mount on your own. Any established move will help, even if it's one you've acquired through practicing the OSP Flashlight Drill for 20 minutes a day the week before the lesson.

What To Do After

Ideally, you have come to the lesson with an open mind and a willingness to learn. If you still have those things when the lesson is over, you're on the road to salvation, Brother. No matter whom you take the lesson from, it's what you do with the information that counts. The most frustrating thing for us is putting our hearts and souls into giving the student all the information they need to improve, and then seeing the student do absolutely nothing with it.

On the flip side, it's a beautiful thing to watch someone take the information gained in a lesson, put it into serious practice, and blossom into a better shooter. When this student comes back for a second lesson and he's undergone a transformation, it makes us want to spend even more time with him, to give him as much as possible. It's the stuff of inspired teaching — a mutually rewarding experience.

So all you really need to do after a lesson is practice what you've learned. Once you understand why it's broke, you can fix it, but you have to practice that fix. If your practice sessions are high quality, your improvement will be high quality. Remember, you are paying for the advice, but it won't do you a lot of good unless you incorporate it into your game through practice.

It's not what you know that makes you better, it's what you are willing to learn. And practice makes the difference.

"What is important for everyone is to look at just the target, to move your eyes to the front edge of the target, and to let the gun go where it wants."

CHAPTER 23
Ladies Only

Ladies, we're glad to have you. Men, you just couldn't resist, could you? You couldn't keep from peeping into the girl's locker room in school, and now you're here. Okay, if you're going to stick around, let's get some things out of the way straight off.

Gentlemen, we know it's difficult, but please don't offer advice to women when they're shooting unless they ask you for it. Actually that goes for everyone, but we find that the ladies are usually the recipients of unsolicited advice — tons of it.

> Remember, free advice will always cost you more than you paid for it!

The camaraderie in shotgunning is special. Everyone wants you to do well. They all wish "powder" for the gal in the box, and advice flows like beer at a fraternity party. They don't realize, though, that they may not be helping. Ladies, if you find yourself getting a lot of free advice we suggest you politely ask the advisor to watch your birds but not offer any thoughts unless asked, because you are trying to coach yourself and self-correct. If you are lost on a target and don't have any idea of how to correct it, ask for suggestions.

Different Perceptions

Another tip for the boys: If you are helping a woman with a shooting problem, you have to understand she doesn't perceive lead like you do. Most men understand a three-foot lead as three feet at the bird. That's why "three feet in front of the bird" has become a common correction. All you guys know what that means, but it doesn't mean the same thing to most ladies.

"Do you mean I should put that little bead three feet in front of the bird? Then why does that put me so far in front? I keep putting that bead three feet in front!" This is the way the dialogue goes until somebody gets frustrated.

Guys, don't tell the ladies to be three feet in front. Most of the time she will literally put three feet of lead on the bird from the barrel, which is actually about 15 to 25 feet in front at the bird. Women see lead in terms of inches at the barrel, not feet at the bird. This doesn't mean that they look at the barrel, it just means that their sight picture is taken in reference to the barrel. They don't see lead like you guys do so please make this easier on everyone and tell them to be one, two, or three inches ahead. Ladies, so that you will understand what the guys are saying, put two targets on the ground three feet apart. Step back 20 yards and hold the gun up on one of the targets. Now look back to the other one. That's what three feet looks like. We all learn in pictures, and this is the picture to remember for all those "three-foot leads."

Remember, it's a guy thing. When we are teaching people how to shoot a teal target, we tell the ladies to look at the bottom of the target, then go to it and pull the trigger. We tell the guys to look at the top of the target. It's just one of the many different

Most men see lead in terms of feet at the target. Almost all women and a few men see lead in terms of inches at the barrel. Regardless of how you see it, it is all perception and rarely do any two people see lead the same.

ways that women and men look at things and it's one of many reasons we try to keep lead out of our instruction. What is important for everyone is: Look at just the target, move your eyes to the front edge of the target, and let the gun go where it wants. It will go to the front automatically and stay in front as long as you keep looking at only the target.

Sharing The Game

The last thing we want to say to the men in this "women's section" is to try not to rush your children or your wives into shotgunning if it's not something they want. For the kids, when they start is more dependent on weight than age. We have found that a child needs to weigh at least 92 pounds. Any smaller and they can't hold up the gun for any length of time. Although there are exceptions be aware that it will only take one bad mount and a lot of recoil and your child's first trip hunting is a bummer.

There is no muscle mass on the shoulder if the weight is not there. The gun will slip out of the shoulder pocket and it will hurt.

We have many fathers who want their children to enjoy hunting like they do, which is wonderful, but let the kids grow into the recoil and the love of the sport.

If your child is under 92 pounds, let him/her come along and see how much fun you can have hunting and shotgunning, but until they are the proper weight, let them bring their BB guns along and play at shooting cans or sticks, or other safe targets.

Often, a husband arranges a lesson for the "little woman" and wants to be right there — just to see that things go well. Gil likes to tell them, "Sure, but it will cost you double to show up and triple if you speak." Jokes aside, if the lady feels the least bit intimidated by having her husband watching, then the answer is "no." If she says it doesn't matter or if she would like him to come then it's OK, but his role is strictly limited. Personally, we like to have the shooting partner there. Partners have a way of communicating in shotgun-shorthand — using their own key words as reminders for focus, gun speed, move and mount, etc. One or two key words are usually all that is needed to correct a miss, but those two words should not include "damn it!"

This Really Is Just For Ladies

One of our first professional successes as an instructing team came about from our work with women in sporting clays. When we first offered up the idea that women perceive lead in an entirely different way than men, many "gurus" in the game said we were crazy. When tons of female shooters began standing up and saying, "No, that is what we see," we suddenly ascended to guru status. And guru-ing is almost as much fun as monkeying!

Perception of lead isn't the only difference. We have found that the ladies are more interested in learning how the process of shooting works. They don't have to hit every target, but they must understand how the gun works, how the shot column works, and how to use their eyes. This all makes sense to them and they understand that hitting the targets will come, but learning how the process works is most important to a woman. The desire to hit the target is there, but it's not their first priority. This is quite different from a typical man's perspective of "I've got to hit that target no matter what. If I load more shells into the gun and shoot more, I'm sure I will hit it eventually." Sound familiar? God, it's fun being a guru!

Ladies, don't let some of those men saddle you with their perception of a good time in sporting clays, which is breaking every target. Once you put pressure on yourself to hit the target, frustration has a way of showing up. Tell the men to let you make the mistakes and correct them without interference. You don't need someone to tell you what to do. We tell our students to make their own corrections and not to rely on anyone else.

Learning Focus

A common question regarding the fairer sex is why they tend to score 10 to 20 fewer targets than men. We've been trying to figure this out for years, since shooting is more a game of finesse than strength. Our thought is that it comes down to one of the biggest differences between men and women: Women have more trouble staying focused on the goal of hitting the target.

Women are used to doing six to 10 things at the same time. Most men do one thing at one time. And they don't have trouble staying focused on one thing. Their only thought while they are in the shooting cage is hitting that target and making it powder. Ladies, what you need to learn — and it is a learned art — is to have all your focus on hitting the target while in the shooting cage. Talk all you want before you get in the shooting cage, but once in there you need to be all business and very focused. Think only of hitting the target, not what others are saying or who has walked up to the station or where you are having dinner tonight.

All that "static" pulls your mind from your objective and makes you lose focus on the game. It's hard to get back to the present. It also creates doubt in your mind that you don't know how to hit the target. Once that doubt enters your mind, you might as well throw your shells in the bushes, because you probably won't hit that target. Have confidence and trust in your ability to hit the targets. Don't let other people make your decisions for you. Get involved in your own decision-making!

Women need to think of the target as the enemy and get a little more assertive about hitting it. When you call for the bird, your whole concentration must be on hitting the target.

We've found that a good way to facilitate this is by tapping into and focusing emotion. When do women become the most focused? When they are angry. A woman gets very focused when she is mad. You can use that to improve your shooting.

The goal for the lady shooter is to find something within herself that triggers assertiveness and makes her so completely focused on hitting that target that she keeps loading her gun until someone tells her to stop.

Don't get frustrated. Get even by becoming focused on nothing but the target. If you can become that focused, your scores will rise.

"The best thing you can do
to improve your game is to perfect your move
and mount and learn to focus on
nothing but the target."

CHAPTER   24
What's missing: the equipment section

You're at the end of the book now, and you might be wondering why we haven't said a word about equipment. What about chokes and loads and gun fit and patterning and gun type? Well, those things are a part of shotgunning and have importance, but they are not the ***most*** important. The best thing you can do to improve your game is to perfect your move and mount and learn to focus on nothing but the target. A quality move and quality focus, these are the most important things to learn initially if you hope to hit clay targets consistently. So in a book about fundamentals, we think it's best not to trouble you with all that crap about equipment.

The equipment is important at advanced levels of shooting, and there will probably come a time when we really get into our experience and advice regarding chokes and loads and gun fit, but that should be done properly and not in one chapter.

Here is our brief recommendation for now: If you're serious about improving at clay sports, get yourself a good pair of shooting glasses, good earplugs, and use a semi-automatic or over-and-under (O/U) target gun, not a side-by-side (SBS). Most SBS guns are intended for game hunting, so they are lightweight and kick. A game gun is intended to be carried a lot and shot a little, while a target gun is intended to be carried a little and shot a lot. Target guns are heavier and have less recoil. If you want to shoot targets, get a target gun.

When you have the proper gun, we suggest you take it to a professional for patterning and a beginner gun fit if you're a novice shooter. What a lot of folks don't know about good gun fit is that it directly relates to your gun mount more than anything else. You can't have perfect gun fit without a perfect move and mount. Gun fit is constantly evolving, and it changes with your skill level and body weight. It might take someone two weeks, two months, or up to two years to get a good gun fit, because if they have no consistency in their move or their mount, they can't expect a consistent fit.

For beginning shooters, we do a beginning gun fit. We determine, as best we can, the correct length of pull and employ enough cast and drop so the shooter can shoot without getting beaten up. After the shooter develops a good move and mount, then and only then, can we make final adjustments to produce a perfect gun fit.

To start off, focus on your move and mount and don't worry so much about gun fit. Although gun fit is important, it is far from the most important thing in successful shooting, and you don't have to have a perfect gun fit to hit targets with a shotgun. Go have fun for now; your familiarity with equipment will come as you journey further into the game.

" Happy shooting. "

CONCLUSION

We hope you enjoyed reading this book as much as we enjoyed writing it.

We're going to conclude by giving you the biggest secret to success in shooting and the secret to our coaching, so all you future coaches pay attention.

First, the secret to success in shooting: In studying and teaching the mental part of this game, it is clear to us that all successful people, regardless of skill, have one thing in common — they have a greater tolerance for failure and setback. They embrace change and learn from failure. If you can do this, you have received a blessing far greater than athleticism. If you give us two beginning students, one with greater athleticism and a bad attitude (inflexible to change), and the other with less athleticism and a good attitude (an open mind/an empty cup), the student with the good attitude will soon be shooting in the 80s, while the more athletic student will be shooting in the 60s.

Now … the secret to our coaching is that we learn as much (if not more) from our students as they do from us. They are the basis for our success, and they are as much our instructors as we are theirs. Experience is the mother of credibility. To be a great shot, one must be experienced at shooting. To be a great teacher, one must be experienced at teaching.

> Technical expertise is always preceded by experience.

Gil was once describing our method of teaching to our son-in-law during a car trip. He said, "The key to teaching is listening. A good teacher will introduce an interrogative and then listen — that's what our instruction is about."

When our son-in-law (one of those "college-edumicated" types) told us that the Greek philosopher Socrates employed this method of teaching over 2,000 years ago, he had no idea what sort of fire he was fueling.

So if on a trip to your local sporting range you see a short guy wearing sandals and a toga and holding a shotgun, don't call the cops. Just go find Vicki and tell her that Gil has finally gone too far.

Happy shooting.